THE HOUDINI SOLUTION

Put Creativity and Innovation to Work by Thinking Inside the Box

ERNIE SCHENCK

New York   Chicago   San Francisco   Lisbon   London   Madrid   Mexico City   Milan   New Delhi   San Juan   Seoul   Singapore   Sydney   Toronto

The *McGraw·Hill* Companies

Library of Congress Cataloging-in-Publication Data

Schenck, Ernie.
    The Houdini solution : put creativity and innovation to work by thinking
inside the box / Ernie Schenck.
        p.   cm.
    Includes index.
    ISBN 0-07-146204-X (alk. paper)
    1. Creative ability in business.   2. Creative thinking.   I. Title.

HD53.S357   2007
658.4'063—dc22   2006020501

1 2 3 4 5 6 7 8 9 10 11 12 13 14 15   DOC/DOC   0 9 8 7 6

ISBN-13: 978-0-07-146204-4
ISBN-10:   0-07-146204-X

McGraw-Hill books are available at special quantity discounts to use as premiums and sales promotions, or for use in corporate training programs. For more information, please write to the Director of Special Sales, Professional Publishing, McGraw-Hill, Two Penn Plaza, New York, NY 10121-2298. Or contact your local bookstore.

This book is printed on acid-free paper.

CONTENTS

Acknowledgments vii

1 Why Thinking Outside the Box Isn't the Answer for Most People 1

2 You See a Wall; Houdini Saw an Opening 9

3 Padlocks, Chains, and Straitjackets: *What's Stopping You from Thinking Creatively?* 25

4 It's Easy to Drown When You're Afraid of Drowning 53

5 He's Been in There for Three Minutes! *The Power of Deadlines* 69

6 Creativity and the Straitjacket of Money 87

7 The Lobsterman and the Lexus 109

8 Thinking Inside the Toy Box 127

9 Houdini Didn't Invent Magic; He Reinvented It 147

10 What? You Thought There Wasn't Going to Be Homework? 165

Afterword 219

Index 223

ACKNOWLEDGMENTS

A lot of people I know think advertising is a huge collaborative effort. I used to be one of them. That was before I started writing a book. Let me tell you something: collaboration in advertising doesn't come close to the kind of close teamwork it takes to get a book written and ultimately published. A lot of people have touched this project along the way, and I am indebted to each of them.

My wife, Rita Lussier. A long time ago, a guy named John Sebastian asked, "Do You Believe in Magic?" I can now honestly say that I do. Without this woman's support and encouragement and especially her inspiration, *The Houdini Solution* would still be in the box.

My kids, Meredith and Geoffrey. They've never let me forget why children think the way they do. I hope they never will.

My agent, Linda Konner, who embraced the project wholeheartedly, who made it better, and to whom I am forever grateful.

My editor at McGraw-Hill, John Aherne, whose talent, enthusiasm, and willingness to listen to the opinionated ramblings of a newbie author are beyond anything I could have asked for.

My advertising buddies all over the world who live the Houdini Solution each and every day. You guys are so amazing.

My personal storytellers. If there were room, I'd list you all. But, of course, even acknowledgment sections have limitations. If you're in the book, you know who you are.

Finally, everyone who ever laid obstacles in my path. Every teacher. Every college professor. Every creative director. Every client. Every one of you who said no when I would much rather have heard yes. I hated you all for a long time. I don't anymore.

Why Thinking Outside the Box Isn't the Answer for Most People

Art lives on constraint and dies of freedom.

—MICHELANGELO

Even for Houdini, it seemed impossible.

Bound and locked in chains, he was to be lowered upside down into a glass box filled with water. He would have minutes to escape. If he succeeded, he would live to see the morning. If he didn't, he would die.

For years Houdini had managed to work his way out of one straitjacket and handcuff after another. But tonight would be different. Tonight he would have to escape death itself.

If it were you, what would you have done? What would you have been thinking as you hung there, suspended in hundreds of gallons of water, surrounded by those six walls of glass, chains clinging heavily against your body, your lungs aching for air?

Unless I miss my bet, I think you would have focused all of your emotional energy on the hopelessness of the situation and quite possibly none of it on finding a solution. I know I would have.

If you were faced with drowning, I think the box would have had you paralyzed with fear. I think you would quickly have resigned yourself to your fate, convinced there was no use in trying to find a way out because the glass was too thick, the water too cold, the chains too tight, the locks too well made.

> Rather than allowing his mind to be *consumed* with the problem, he directed all of his energy toward *solving* it.

But Houdini had a different approach. Instead, he accepted his circumstances. He accepted the box. He accepted the water inside the box. He accepted the chains and the locks. Rather than allowing his mind to be *consumed* with the problem, he directed all of his energy toward *solving* it.

This is what I call the Houdini Solution.

It's pretty simple, and I believe that if more people followed Houdini's example of accepting their own personal life boxes, whatever those might be, they could tap into an enormous reservoir of personal creativity. And believe me, it's there.

Maybe you don't think of yourself as a particularly creative person. Or maybe you do. Maybe you think there's a life-altering new product idea in you. Or a groundbreaking brand extension. Maybe a book, even a screenplay. But because you live on a tree-lined street in the suburbs with three kids, two cars, a dog, and a mortgage, you assume you just don't have the kind of freedom that's conducive to leading a creative life.

But you're wrong.

Life Is a Box: Deal with It

Think outside the box. Year after year, in book after book, that's what we've been told by one self-styled creativity guru after another. The message was clear. If we wanted to free ourselves to think creatively, there could be no walls, no barriers, no rules or constrictions of any kind.

Somehow we had to get out of our ruts, divorce ourselves from the humdrum rhythm of our lives, take our minds to a different place, where the real world could be set aside, ignored, freeze-framed. If only we could free ourselves, if only we could climb out of that infernal box, they told us, we could discover our true creative selves.

And yet for millions of us, those boxes are very real. Almost everything in our lives is a box. Our relationships. Our jobs. Where we live. How young or old we are. Our bank accounts. They're all boxes. They all have walls. They all have boundaries. But they are not all bad.

Maybe you're married. If so, there are probably lines that neither you nor your partner would consider crossing—that is, not unless you're willing to accept some sort of consequence. Myself, I know that if I decide to borrow from the 401(k) to buy, say, a dirt bike—well, my wife might have a little problem with that. And if she donates my old college sweatshirt to Goodwill without telling me—again, we're going to have words.

How about your job? Big box. Huge box. There are time sheets to be filled out, sales quotas to be met, work spaces to be tolerated. Maybe you've got a coworker who's really obnoxious. Maybe your boss is a total bully. Maybe you aren't paid anywhere near what you're worth but feel you can't say anything because another job would mean moving halfway across the country and you can't do that because your elderly mother doesn't want to leave her apartment and since you're the only child, who else is going to look after her?

You think people are the only ones who have to deal with boxes? Think again. Entire countries exist inside boxes. The walls can be many: poverty, social unrest, harsh climates, hostile neighbors, immigration problems, trade embargoes, shrinking currencies, dictatorships. Just like people, countries can choose to accept their lot in the world or they can work to find creative ways to flourish, not by ridding themselves of the limitations that define them but by embracing them.

> Entire countries exist inside boxes.

Blessed with some of the most spectacular terrain on the planet, New Zealand nonetheless is a relatively isolated country, tens of thousands of miles from most of the world's vacationers and long regarded as a great place to visit, assuming you're a shepherd. In New Zealand's case, its box was defined by all these soaring mountains and lush, green valleys that, beautiful though they might be, weren't exactly getting it done in the tourism arena. But then came the *Lord of the Rings* trilogy. Filmed in New Zealand, the movies were an enormous success, and, thinking inside the box, the country quickly began promoting itself as the land of the hobbit. Suddenly people were coming from all over the world to see the dark land of Mordor, the summit of Amon Hen, and the Ford of Bruinen—in other words, those same mountains, lakes, and valleys that had been there all along. New Zealand might not know it, but the country is a textbook example of the Houdini Solution.

Think Hollywood doesn't exist in a box? Sure it does. Several years ago I attended a screenwriting workshop run by Robert McKee called Story Structure. You can pretty much guess the overarching premise of the class from its title. McKee made it pretty clear. The story at the core of every really great movie works within the concrete boundaries of a defined architecture. Abandon that architecture, and you will have a film that, with the exception of maybe a few people in black clothes and goatees in Greenwich Village, virtually no one will care much to see. And what about the studios? Think they're out-of-the-box thinkers? Please. It's the rare movie executive these days who's willing to stick his or her neck out to greenlight a quirky, offbeat little film like, say, *My Big Fat Greek Wedding*, when everybody knows what people really want is exploding police cars, killer cyborgs, and volcanoes erupting in Los Angeles.

Madison Avenue might be a long way from Hollywood, but it isn't far behind. I'm a copywriter and a creative director. That means I basically write print ads and TV commercials for a living, or if I'm not doing the actual writing, I'm managing people who are. Sounds like fun, right? There aren't many jobs where you actually get paid to sit around all day thinking up funny TV commercials. But let me tell you, for a business whose very existence is ostensibly rooted in creative thinking, advertising is very much a box, too. Clients can be enormously opinionated. There are deadlines. You have to create on demand. There are things you can't say, things you can't show. As creative as this industry is, we are very much bound by our boxes.

Muse, Shmuse

The point is, like it or not, most of us are stuck with the circumstances in which we find ourselves. And those circumstances have parameters—undeniable limitations that we either can't change or could change but don't wish to.

> Limitations are like the banks of a river. Without them, the river becomes a formless mass without direction.

Contrary to what you might believe, this is not a bad thing. Limitations are like the banks of a river. Without them, the river becomes instead a formless mass without direction, just sort of spreading out everywhere but going nowhere.

The psychologist Rollo May puts it this way: "Creativity requires limits, for the creative act arises out of the struggle of human beings and against that which limits them."

For millions of people hungry to lead more creative, more innovative lives, the real question therefore isn't

"How can I become more creative?" It's "How can I become more creative within the confines of my life?"

The good news is that, contrary to everything you've heard, you really can lead a more creative life despite all of it. I don't care what you've been taught. I don't care what you've been conditioned to believe. You can think more creatively right now. Without running off to an artist colony. Without disengaging from your responsibilities. Without waiting for some fictional muse that doesn't exist and never did.

It really is true. We're all creative. I believe that we human beings are an inherently creative species. We could never have gotten to where we are if this were not true. All of our greatest achievements can be traced back to a single moment when someone added two and two and got five. The pyramids. Einstein's theory of relativity. The light bulb. Quantum physics. The polio vaccine. Mickey Mouse. Spider-Man. Harry Potter.

And believe me, it's not just the Thomas Edisons and the Jonas Salks and the Walt Disneys of the world who have this wonderful capability. You don't have to be a painter or a novelist or a composer. I don't care if you're a cattle rancher, a NASA flight engineer, or a bank teller. You are a fundamentally creative person with a power to innovate, and once you know how to tap into that power, it can change your life forever.

> Human beings are an inherently creative species.

By the time you have finished *The Houdini Solution*, if you have learned one thing, it will be this: the biggest secret of truly productive creative people is that they embrace obstacles, they don't run from them. In their minds every setback is an opportunity, every limitation is a chance. Where others see a wall, they see a doorway.

The Houdini Solution will show you that the true path to creativity lies not outside, but *inside*, the box, and it is only when we are confronted with boundaries that we are able to unleash the full force of our creative potential.

You See a Wall; Houdini Saw an Opening

Houston, we've had a problem.
—Jack Swigert, Apollo 13

On the night of April 15, 1970, Ed Smylie was at home watching TV when he got the news. There had been an explosion aboard Apollo 13, and could he please get down to the Houston Space Center as quickly as possible.

Minutes later, Smylie, who at the time oversaw NASA's crew systems division, learned that the spacecraft was slowly losing oxygen, electricity, light, and water some 200,000 miles from the Earth.

To make matters worse, there was a problem with the lithium dioxide canisters, whose job it was to cleanse carbon dioxide from the air. While the spare canisters from the command module were square, the openings in the lunar module environment control system were round. Unless Smylie and his staff could design a way to make the square canisters compatible with the round holes using only materials available aboard the crippled spacecraft, the crew would die of asphyxiation within a day or two.

If there is a better example of the Houdini Solution than what those NASA engineers were able to pull off in the next forty-eight hours, I don't know what it could be. Talk about thinking inside the box. You've got to design a new product. You've got to build that product. Your raw materials consist of cardboard, plastic bags, duct tape, and other low-tech materials. And, hey, just for good measure, you've got less than forty-eight hours to do it or people are going to die.

But that's exactly what that tiny group of NASA engineers did on that fateful night. Instead of allowing the limitations of the situation to control them, they embraced them. Yes, the walls were closing in. Yes, the sense of claustrophobia had to be overwhelming. And yet they somehow were able to find an ingenious solution.

What if those same engineers had had weeks instead of hours to solve the same problem? What do you suppose would have happened? Would they have found a solution? Of course, they would have. These were NASA engineers, for crying out loud. They don't come any smarter. So, yes, they would have solved the problem. The real question is, would it have been any more *creative* than that little contraption they cobbled together under enormous pressure? I doubt it.

In essence, the Houdini Solution is really a form of creative judo. If you know anything about the martial arts, you know that judo is a way to defend yourself against attackers by using their own strength against them. Unlike boxing, where you fight back, in judo it's just the opposite. You accept the power of your enemy. You let it wash over you. You do not resist it in any way. You simply let it come at you, and then you leverage that power in a way that works on your behalf. This is what it's like to think inside the box.

> The Houdini Solution is really a form of creative judo.

In the early 1990s Chevys was one of the largest Mexican food restaurant chains in America. It prided itself on its "fresh Mex" food, and when it turned to San Francisco ad agency Goodby Berlin Silverstein to handle its advertising, Chevys had just one message it wanted to communicate: everything on Chevys' menu is made fresh each and every day.

Steve Simpson and Tracy Wong were the creative team assigned to Chevys, and the idea they came up with remains one of the biggest, most elegant examples of Houdini Solution thinking I have ever encountered.

The budget they had to work with for Chevys wasn't exactly in the same league as for, say, McDonald's or General Motors, so any idea that depended on shooting for three weeks with an A-list director on some South Pacific island with Michael Jordan and a couple dozen Rockettes wasn't in the cards. The problem was clear. How could Chevys convince consumers that its food was made fresh every day and do that on a budget smaller than the contents of Budweiser's petty cash drawer?

Armed with a simple video camera, Simpson and Wong got up every day at the crack of dawn, went out into the streets where they would ask real people if they were aware that Chevys made their food fresh every day, got some surprisingly funny answers, rushed back to the office, and edited the film so the finished spots could air that same night on TV. Nobody had ever done that before.

"Necessity is the mother of invention," says Wong. "We had a boring, almost generic strategy. We had no money. No director would touch the assignment. And we had to shoot what turned out to be four to five commercials a month. We were screwed by both the strategy and the budget, thank God. It forced us to do what we did."

The Chevys campaign was truly groundbreaking, and it worked like gangbusters. The effect was, hey, if even the TV commercials are fresh, imagine what the food must taste like. Brilliant. And it might never have happened if Simpson and Wong hadn't been forced to work inside, instead of outside, the box.

The idea that all the limitations that we've come to believe are inhibitors of creative thinking could, in fact, be the liberators of it is, of course, extremely counterintuitive. But that is exactly what they are. And once you discover that, once you learn how to use those limitations to your advantage instead of allowing them to muffle the potential of your company, the possibilities are just enormous.

Nobody knows this better than Daniel Myrick and Eduardo Sànchez. In 1999 their little black-and-white faux documentary about three young filmmakers who set off into the woods near Burkittsville, Maryland, in search of a mythical witch became one of the most profitable films in history. By all accounts, *The Blair Witch Project*, made for a paltry $50,000 or so, should never have gone on to gross $140 million. *Star Wars: Episode I—The Phantom Menace*, which came out that same year with its production budget in excess of $115 million, was nowhere near as profitable. In fact, it's probably safe to say that *Phantom* spent more on lunch for its production crew than Myrick and Sanchez had for their entire movie. And money wasn't the only barrier. To the Hollywood establishment, the two young filmmakers were total unknowns. Two snot-nosed ciphers. Just a couple of film school wannabes with a lot of ambition and not much else. So they didn't have any connections. No friend of a producer or a talent agent or even a studio electrician. Needless to say, Brad Pitt wasn't available. Nor was George Clooney or Julia Roberts. Finding a distributor was about as likely to happen as finding a two-headed monkey on Wall Street, although the film eventually did find a home with Artisan Entertainment. Yes, there was a marketing budget. Kind of. But certainly it wasn't even close to what the majors were used to spending. Truth to tell, there wasn't even a script, just a loose plot structure that required the film's actors to pretty much improvise their dialogue.

And yet, despite it all, *The Blair Witch Project* went on to become one of the most successful movies of all time. Why? Because like Houdini, instead of allowing the box to defeat them, Myrick and Sanchez accepted it. Worked with it. Cooperated with it. Let it shape and bend and mold their vision into something it would have never become if they hadn't understood the power of the Houdini Solution. In a

1999 interview with Salon.com, when asked if he thought the effectiveness of *Blair Witch* was because of that filmmaking process, first-time actor Joshua Leonard was quick to reply. "Absolutely. Sony could have $50 million and a soundstage and A-list actors and never make the same film. The constraints on this film became the essence of this film, which became the power of this film."

You wouldn't think *The Blair Witch Project* and Bang & Olufsen have much in common, but they do. In July of 2003 the Danish consumer electronics firm was getting ready to launch a new line of $17,000 speakers. To get it off the ground, they decided to do a special event for their best customers and prospects in Chicago. But like Myrick and Sanchez, the company was working with extremely limited funds. Thinking *inside* the box, B&O built a series of partnerships with luxury brands, giving it a ready-made guest list consisting of 160 handpicked platinum card members, each of whom was picked up in a Bentley and driven by chauffeur to the Chicago store for a demonstration, then to drinks and dinner at NoMI, one of the hottest and chicest restaurants in the city. NoMI paid for much of the food, and Bentley certainly was willing to cooperate, seeing how it had 160 potential customers out riding around in Bentleys all night. By all accounts, the event was an unmitigated success in bringing together passionately loyal B&O fans with potential new customers. Best of all, the entire event cost Bang & Olufsen virtually nothing to produce. Like the Chevys fresh-Mex campaign and *The Blair Witch Project*, the Bang & Olufsen event was successful because the company, instead of trying to swim against the tide of a limited budget, was smart enough to let itself be shaped by it.

There's No Such Thing as a Dumb Question. Or Is There?

So why is it that some people are defeated by constraints and others are seemingly energized by them? How are companies like Bang & Olufsen able to navigate their way through a minefield of limitations so effortlessly, while that very same minefield can leave other companies so creatively constipated?

Creativity is like a nuclear reactor. And like any nuclear reactor, it can't generate electricity until something gets a chain reaction going. When it comes to thinking inside the box, nothing gets that reaction going like asking questions.

> Creativity is like a nuclear reactor. And like any nuclear reactor, it can't generate electricity until something gets a chain reaction going.

Here's what I mean. Imagine you and I are sitting at a table. I put a pie down in front of you. I give you a knife. Then I ask you to pick up the knife and cut the pie into eight pieces using three cuts. In other words, I put you in a box. Not unexpectedly, most people drive themselves nuts making three straight cuts in all kinds of ways, not one of which will result in eight pieces. The reason is that most people just start cutting. They don't ask questions first. They just assume that there are only so many ways one can cut a pie using only three cuts and end up with eight pieces. But in the world of the Houdini Solution, you would have tested the limits of the box by asking questions, like "Do the lines have to be cut from the top of the pie down through to the bottom?" If the answer were no, then you might have thought to cut the pie into fourths, then slice the entire pie horizontally. Or maybe you might have asked, "Do all the cuts have to be straight?" Well, did I say that they did? No, I didn't. I simply said to cut the pie into eight pieces using three cuts. That said, a second idea would have been to cut the pie into fourths and then make a third, vertical but circular cut halfway out from the center of the pie. Both solutions are pretty innovative. And yet if you didn't ask questions, your own assumptions of how a pie is normally cut would blind you to any kind of creative solution.

I must warn you though. Questions can lead you as easily to the wrong solution as they can to the right one. The trick is to ask the *right* questions. Volvo almost learned this the hard way when a single wrong question nearly spelled disaster for one of the world's most respected car companies.

> The trick is to ask the *right* questions.

Unless you've been living in a cave for the last twenty years or so, you know that Volvo has been virtually joined at the hip with the concept of safety. You think of Volvo, you think of safety. Not performance. Not sexy styling. Not fuel efficiency. Safety. For years Volvo nurtured that single-minded position, never veering from it, never losing its focus. Consumers had this drilled into their heads over and over again. If it wasn't the reinforced steel beams in the car's roof, it was the side panel airbags. The advertising featured crash survivors who testified to their belief that their Volvos had saved their lives. If safety was more important to you than anything else in a car, then you had to consider a Volvo. You just had to.

But then something started happening. Other cars started coming out with the same safety features as Volvo. Little by little, Volvo's long-running domination of the kingdom of safe cars was eroding. Or so the company believed. So Volvo started asking questions. "What can we be that we're not now?" "Is it time we started migrating to some other position besides safety?" "Could we start selling our cars on, say, style or performance?"

The result was that for the first time in decades, Volvo began to push performance. Never mind that no driver in his or her right mind would ever utter "Volvo" and "BMW" in the same breath. Surely, in its heart of hearts, the company had to have known this. But Volvo never took the time to question the questions. All it knew was that other car companies were starting to encroach on safety, and so it was only a matter of time before Volvo would be stripped of the one thing it had always been known for. And if that happened, the brand might never recover. Something had to be done. And something was.

Instead of the boxy tanks that had helped reinforce the car's reputation for safety, the cars now were beginning to look sleeker, more stylish. Less like the stodgy bank vault and more like something that could be very much at home on, say, the autobahn. The new look said, "Hey, look at us. We're sleek. We're fast. We're sexy."

Volvo had asked the wrong questions.

As Anne E. Bélec, president and chief executive at Volvo Cars North America, said in a speech to the American Association of Advertising Agencies in 2005, "The approach was an ill-suited and therefore ill-fated detour into using performance as a selling strategy, which strayed too far from the Volvo brand identity."

Again, Volvo jumped ship on the ill-fated strategy almost as quickly as it had conceived it. But this time around, the company asked the right questions. "Why should we try to be something we're not?" "Why should we walk away from what's made us successful?" "Instead, is there something we can do to spin the idea of safety off in a slightly different direction?"

The result is that Volvo returned to its message of safety but this time with a new twist that took the brand into more emotional territory. This time, it wasn't just "Volvo. Drive Safely." It was "Volvo. For Life." It was a subtle shift in strategy, but an effective one. It dusted off Volvo's message and dressed it up in new clothes and in at least one commercial managed to work in the new performance strategy at the same time. Maybe you remember it. In the Xbox video game *RalliSport Challenge 2*, a red Volvo S40 is barreling over twisty roads, powersliding around curves, and finally ends up rolling down a hill in a mind-popping crash. No way could someone survive an accident like that. And yet, a second later, the driver climbs out none the worse for wear. After all, he was driving a Volvo. It was very effective. Not only did it reinforce Volvo's reputation for safety in an outrageously new and cool way, but the hair-raising rally car action screamed performance. Ingenious. And it happened because Volvo ultimately saw the wisdom in thinking inside, not outside, the box.

They Don't Call It Mind-Bending for Nothing

When people truly embrace the Houdini Solution, they begin to look at the box differently. Where others see a prison cell, Houdini companies see creative opportunities. Where most organizations and people feel crushed under the weight of all the reasons why they can't be innovative, Houdini thinkers feel nothing of the sort, knowing with absolute certainty that if they engage the box, if they lock onto it, touch it, feel its closeness, an innovative solution will reveal itself. Just as it did for Tracy Wong and Steve Simpson. Just as it did for Bang & Olufsen and Volvo.

So what makes the difference? What is it about Houdini thinkers that enables them to come up with so many innovative ideas? Without ignoring reality. Without setting one department off against the other. Without standing the corporate culture on its ear. Without doing something fatally stupid. While there are many factors, the single most glaring difference between companies that use the box as an excuse to maintain the status quo and those that use it to drive the company forward is flexibility. When you're working in a confined space whose walls are determined by an immovable set of boundaries, the more flexible you are, the more you can roll with the circumstances, the more likely it is that a big idea will reveal itself.

In 1950 Ray Bradbury, the highly lauded author of *Dandelion Wine, Fahrenheit 451*, and *Something Wicked This Way Comes*, had just published *The Martian Chronicles* and was working on his next book, *The Illustrated Man*. Like most of Bradbury's works, the new book was originally intended to be a collection of short stories. But Bradbury's editor felt the book would do better as a novel. Was there some way, the editor wondered, that Ray might be able to convert what were essentially completely different stories?

A lot of writers would have said, no way. Impossible. The stories have no relation to each other. The characters are all different. There'd be no cohesive plot line. It just wouldn't make any sense. It's just not possible. A lot of writers would have said that. But Ray Bradbury was different. After all, this was the same man whose entire life had been spent imagining time machines and rocket ships and colonies on Mars. It was possible.

Obviously, if you've read *The Illustrated Man*, then you know how Ray solved this seemingly unsolvable problem. But if you haven't, then take a minute and think about this one. What would you have done? Again, consider the box Ray found himself in. You've worked for months writing what you thought was going to be a collection of short stories. The stories are unrelated. The characters are all different. There is no single protagonist. There is no single plot line. And then comes the kicker. Your editor wants you to turn your short stories into a novel. Give up?

OK, here's how Bradbury did it.

He had written a short story called *The Illustrated Man*. While his editor decided to pass on the story, he liked the title. Even though the story wasn't going to make the cut, Ray thought maybe there might be a way to use the main character in a prologue to the novel that would more or less set up a narrative device that would glue all the different stories together. In the prologue, with the story line continuing in several other short transitional chapters that kept the narrative going throughout the book, a young wanderer meets an out-of-work carnival performer whose body is covered with tattoos. The young wanderer quickly discovers that each tattoo is in reality a vision of some future event as told by each of the short stories. Suddenly, the stories related. Where there had been no protagonist, now there was. Where there had been no common narrative thread, now there was. It was pure genius. And yet if Ray Bradbury hadn't been creatively flexible, would it have happened?

I think I know what Jack White's answer would be.

Where Creative Limits Don't Exist, Create Them

Jack is a guitarist and songwriter and the leader of the Grammy Award–winning rock band White Stripes. As rock musicians go, Jack White is something of a contrarian. Born in 1975, White is a throwback to a simpler, purer form of rock and roll. In that sense he shares more with the likes of Neil Young, Pearl Jam, and Frank Zappa than he does with his contemporaries. For the most part, the Houdini Solution is about accepting the box and working inside it. White takes this one step further. Instead of working *around* creative obstacles, Jack *invents* them. So severe are these self-imposed restrictions, they border on the monastic. No computers. No digital recording technology. No bass guitars. No studio equipment invented after 1968. No clothes that aren't red, white, or black. It's a kind of forced creative captivity that nurtures innovation and strives for a form of music that's far more rooted in talent than it is in technology.

> For the most part, the Houdini Solution is about accepting the box and working inside it.

Jack White isn't the only musician who believes in the power of imposed creative restraints. Brian Eno once devised a set of role-playing exercises that he later had printed onto a deck of cards, which he called the Oblique Strategies. Each card had printed on it a limitation, or role, the artist had to assume before performing. In this sense, it was much like improv comedy where the comedian must spontaneously ad-lib a routine without any previous preparation. Allegedly, when Eno was producing David Bowie's album *Outside*, Eno gave each member of Bowie's band one of the strategies and instructed them to embrace it during the recording session. So, for example, the lead guitarist might have been told to play as if he had just escaped from a totalitarian regime that had forbidden him to play specific notes and riffs, and now that he was free, he could play *only* those notes and riffs and no others. The effect was that by limiting the band's creativity, Eno had in fact done just the opposite.

Running a business or living your life, of course, isn't like playing in a rock band. Still, you have more in common with White Stripes and Brian Eno than you think. You see a connection between limitations and creativity. Jack White sees a connection between limitations and creativity. You know what it feels like to work inside a box, Brian Eno knows what it's like to work inside a box. The difference is, you see limitations as a roadblock to innovation. White Stripes, on the other hand, reveres them. You think the box is a bad thing. Brian Eno sees nothing but good. Believe me when I tell you, there is a lesson to be learned from Jack White and Brian Eno, and the sooner you learn it, the sooner you'll begin to realize that inside every wall lies a secret passageway that leads to all sorts of extraordinary opportunities.

> Inside every wall lies a secret passageway that leads to all sorts of extraordinary opportunities.

Padlocks, Chains, and Straitjackets

What's Stopping You from Thinking Creatively?

When forced to work within a strict framework, the imagination is taxed to its utmost and will produce its richest ideas.

—T. S. Eliot

The last person on earth Hereward Carrington expected to see in the audience that night was Harry Houdini, and Carrington wasn't pleased.

The two men had been friends once, but that was before the ugliness with Margery Crandon. Things hadn't been the same between them since then.

A purported medium with psychic abilities, Crandon had created quite a stir within the Scientific American Committee, of which both Carrington and Houdini were members. After a prolonged investigation, it was the committee's conclusion that Crandon was, in fact, a fake.

But the vote hadn't been unanimous, with Carrington the only member who steadfastly insisted that Crandon was the real thing.

If Houdini and the others suspected that Carrington's position had been driven by something else besides mere conviction, it wouldn't have been surprising. Carrington had recently taken to representing a number of psychics at staged performances in the United States.

This night it was a twenty-six-year-old Egyptian named Rahman Bey. It was said that Bey was capable of extraordinary physical feats, some of which bordered on the supernatural, but none so extraordinary as tonight's performance in which the young Egyptian would emerge from an airtight coffin after being shut inside for more than ten minutes. He claimed this was possible because he was able to put himself into what he called "a cataleptic trance," thereby putting his body into a state of suspended animation.

But Houdini wasn't buying it. Convinced that Bey's seemingly miraculous escape from death was nothing more than a cheap trick, Houdini vowed to perform the same escape, remaining in the same coffin for as long as Bey, only there would be no trances.

Bey lost no time raising the stakes, duplicating his escape mere days later, when he managed to stay in the coffin, submerged at the bottom of a swimming pool, this time for longer than one hour.

Houdini would now have to make good on his promise. But how? Even Houdini knew the odds were not in his favor. At just twenty-six years of age, Bey was young. Houdini was fifty-two. Bey was thin and weighed very little. Houdini was considerably heavier and not exactly at the height of his physical powers. It was a difference that would loom large for Houdini, and he knew it.

Nonetheless, on August 5, 1926, after being examined by a team of physicians with hundreds of reporters looking on, the aging Houdini climbed into a galvanized iron coffin, which was promptly sealed and lowered into the swimming pool of the Hotel Shelton in New York City.

No one there that day expected Houdini to survive more than three minutes. Biologically, three minutes was considered the outer limit of the average human being's lung capacity. That was the conventional wisdom. And as is true of most conventional wisdom, most people tended to accept it as fact.

But Houdini saw it differently.

Yes, the scant volume of air in the coffin was an obstacle. So was his age and his lack of conditioning. But maybe those obstacles weren't as daunting as they seemed. Unquestionably, there was only so much air to breathe, and at some point his physical limits would indeed become a factor. There was nothing he could do to manufacture more air or make himself younger. All this was true.

But even if he couldn't change the limitations, what if he could change his *attitude* toward those limitations? It was no different than a game of poker, Houdini reasoned. He had been dealt a hand, and that hand was a defined amount of air, a fifty-two-year-old body, and a woeful lack of conditioning. What if he could do a better job at playing that hand? Might that be the key?

Apparently, it was.

After one hour and twenty-eight minutes and much to the amazement of the world, Harry Houdini emerged from the bottom of the Hotel Shelton pool, not only alive but, with the exception of looking a bit pale, feeling relatively well. The skeptics, of course, insisted it was a trick. But a rigorous examination of the coffin was unable to detect even the slightest amount of evidence that Houdini had somehow managed to pipe in an external supply of air. As he would later write, "Anyone could have done it."

But is that true?

Could anyone have done it? Could anyone have had the ability to stare into the mouth of panic and see a possibility? Could anyone have had the discipline to lie perfectly still in a sealed, iron coffin at the bottom of a swimming pool, taking breaths so shallow they were barely perceptible? Could anyone have, instead of looking at the walls of that coffin and seeing a death trap, seen an opportunity? I don't think many of us could.

We All Fear Barriers, and Why Wouldn't We?

All our lives, most of us are taught that barriers are a bad thing. They get in our way. They keep us from being here and getting there. Barriers spell problems, and if we can avoid problems, this is a good thing. This isn't to say that we don't deal with problems every day. We do. But if a problem can be avoided, why would we not do that?

Creativity is one of those problems.

It's a paradox, I know. After all, unless you've been living on a desert island for the last several years, you know that the ability of companies to innovate has become the new coin of the corporate realm. Doesn't matter if you make mainframes or fertilizer, run a cruise line or a newspaper. Whether you're in business or the arts, you're in the business of ideas. You innovate or you die. Period.

> You innovate or you die. Period.

The problem is that a lot of companies and people are scared to death of creativity. And it's not difficult to see why. While innovation means giving birth to something new, it also means killing off something old. At the very least, old ways of doing things are disturbed. Shaken up. Knocked out of their delicate orbits. And if you're running a company, this is not something you want to hear. On the one hand, you know that brilliant ideas can take a business or an aspect of your life to dizzying heights it's never known before. But then there's that damned other hand. The one that says, "Yes, but what if you're wrong? Just because an idea is big doesn't mean it can't hurt us. Look at Godzilla. He was big. And look what happened to Tokyo."

I'm in advertising. Creativity is what I'm all about. I believe in it. I've seen it accomplish spectacular, breathtaking, amazing things. I've seen it bring dead brands back to life faster than Lazarus, and I'm not exaggerating. Creativity is an incredibly powerful thing. And I'd love to tell you that your fears are unfounded, that creativity is the key to everything, and if only you would, as Yoda suggested, trust in the force, you would not be sorry.

I'd like to tell you that. But I can't.

Arguably, few companies in history have built their culture around innovation more than Apple Computer. From the very beginning, Apple has displayed an almost obsessive penchant for creativity and groundbreaking technology matched by few companies in any sector, let alone high technology. Time and again, Apple has led the way with products that even its harshest critics have applauded as being among some of the most elegant in the known universe.

"Innovate," Steve Jobs has said. "That's what we do."

Yes, it is. And yet, for all its ingenuity, for all its single-minded and dogged pursuit of innovative purity, Apple continues to be a relatively bit player compared with its less creatively driven competitors.

At one time, Xerox's Palo Alto Research Center (PARC) was a virtual wonderland of human ingenuity that ultimately led to the laser printer, the mouse pointing device, and the Ethernet. And while Steve Jobs and Apple might have developed the graphical user interface, the concept is widely considered to have originated at PARC. Like Apple, PARC was creatively on fire. For PARC, the problem wasn't thinking outside the box. It was making money. The place never made a nickel.

I can still remember the first time I shot a Polaroid camera. It was unbelievable. You shot a picture and out it came sixty seconds later. It was one of those "wow" moments that just shake you to the core with their brilliance. Polaroid had success written all over it. How could it miss with an outside-the-box idea like instant photography? It couldn't. Yet in October of 2001, that's exactly what happened when the company finally went Chapter 11.

No Idea Is More Dangerous than Not Having One

Creativity is a powerful thing. But it's not perfect. Nothing is. Despite all the wonderful things creativity has achieved, and there are many, it's also been responsible for some genuine bombs, the likes of which make a daisy cutter bomb look like a firecracker.

Before 1985 Coca-Cola was the undisputed king of soft drinks. Although Pepsi had been steadily gaining market share on Coke, Coca-Cola still had the pole position in the cola race. Then something extraordinary happened. People started hoarding Coke. On the black market, it was going for $30 a case. Some loyal fans began having it overnighted to them from Montreal. There's a story that one Hollywood producer shelled out $1,200 to rent a wine cellar to store more than a hundred cases of Coke.

You know why?

Because in April of 1985, Coca-Cola decided that if it was going to staunch the bleeding inflicted on it by the Pepsi assault, it was going to have to get creative. And they did. The result was called New Coke. Reactions from loyal Coke drinkers were swift and harsh, likening the new formula to sewer water, furniture polish, and two-day old

Pepsi. "Changing Coke," one respondent said, "is like God making the grass purple." Another put it this way, "Next week, they'll be chiseling Teddy Roosevelt off the side of Mount Rushmore." To say that New Coke was one of the more hideous consequences of outside-the-box innovation is putting it mildly.

As Sergio Zyman, the former chief marketing officer of Coca-Cola, puts it, "Pepsi was telling consumers that Coke was fat, lazy and an outdated way of drinking cola, and they offered the Pepsi Challenge to prove it. Rather than address the value proposition problem, we opted for the easy way out. We decided we needed to innovate, so we changed the formula to make Coke taste more like Pepsi."

Few people at Coca-Cola didn't have high hopes for New Coke. At the time, it seemed like a good idea. A creative idea. Yet it was a gargantuan failure. And although Coca-Cola managed to get back on its feet quickly, returning to Classic Coke within seven months of New Coke's ill-fated launch, it learned a powerful lesson: without boundaries, without knowing what they are, where they are, what they're made of, how they're shaped, how high they are, how low, how thick, what they taste like, what they feel like, how they're perceived in the real world, without accepting that they exist, innovation can be a dangerous thing.

In the end, creativity is like anything else in life. It doesn't come with a guarantee. It might work. It might not. And if it doesn't, it can leave a company worse off than before. Sometimes, a lot worse.

I'm going to say it again. Creativity can be a destructive act. And if that scares you, it should. What happens if the big idea doesn't work out? Sure, like Coca-Cola, maybe it won't be too late to bring the old way back. But what if it were your company? Your life? What if you committed so much to the new that going back to the old just wasn't an option? Not only could it be time-consuming, it could, and probably would, be mind-numbingly expensive if not downright lethal.

But here's the thing. As risky as creativity can be, stagnation is worse. A lot worse. Do something new, and maybe it'll backfire. Do nothing new, and it will eventually blow up in your face. The promise of the Houdini Solution is that there's a third way. A way of building creativity that doesn't ask you to choose between black and white, that doesn't make

> As risky as creativity can be, stagnation is worse.

you feel like a trapeze artist working without a net. I know it works because I've seen it work. I've been practicing the principles of the Houdini Solution for more than twenty years, and let me tell you, if they can work on Madison Avenue, where advertising agencies live and die on their creative product, trust me—they'll work for you, too.

So what about it? Other than a natural aversion to risk, what specifically is standing between the person you are or the company you are and the company and person you could be? It's an important question, and you need to answer it.

As you know by now, *The Houdini Solution* is about thinking inside, not outside, the box. But before I can show you how to do that, you've got to know those walls like you know your own kids. You've got to know where they are and what they are. You've got to know every nook, every cranny, every crack, and every pockmark—and you've got to know them cold.

Ancient Greece Had Its Mythology; So Does Creativity

So exactly how do you do that?

It's true that there are as many reasons for people and companies to avoid thinking creatively as there are, well, people and companies. This is inarguable. But what I can tell you from my experience with hundreds of brands in dozens of industries from cars to software to sporting goods to life insurance is that when you boil it down, there are fourteen barriers to creativity that loom higher than all the rest. And these barriers exist in both your personal and professional lives.

Understand those barriers, and you understand the box. Understand the box, and you understand how to embrace it, how to work with it and to turn it from the prison you perceive it to be into the gaping doorway to truly creative thinking that it actually is.

MYTH #1: CREATIVITY IS FOR CREATIVE PEOPLE

You'd think that in an advertising agency, creativity would be expected in every nook and cranny. And that's true. As long as those nooks and crannies are in the creative department. Sure, account planners can have an idea. So can a media buyer. So can the kid in the mailroom. And sometimes they do. But for all its creative sophistication, advertising still pretty much sees the creative process as the province of the creatives. Which as a job description always seemed pretty exclusionary to me.

The thing is, if one of the most creatively driven industries in all of business can confine creativity to an elite category of people, it's understandable that other businesses would do the same. But that is such a monstrous mistake.

Maybe you think a CPA can't have a creative idea. And why wouldn't you? CPAs are left-brain people. They crunch numbers. They add. They subtract. They multiply and divide. End of story.

But believe it or not, CPAs actually have a right brain, too. Just like the rest of us. And that means they have the ability to make the kind of connections between seemingly unrelated thoughts that are at the heart of all innovation. You might not think they do. *They* might not even think they do. But it's there. It just needs to be tapped. Set free. Set loose upon the world.

I once had the AICPA for a client. American Institute of Certified Public Accountants. Sounds boring, right? I know I thought so. Nevertheless, my partner and I worked for weeks coming up with dozens of ideas for campaigns that we thought were spot on. Then came the day of the presentation. To say it was an unmitigated train wreck would be putting it mildly. The client hated everything. When the smoke finally cleared, we were sitting in the conference room with a couple of lower-level executives from their side who'd taken pity on us and were trying to comfort us with stuff like "I think you're close" and "I didn't think that went so bad." But it did go bad. Worse than bad. And even worse than that, we only had two weeks before our first insertion dates. We were screwed. But then one of these guys came out with a thought. He just laid it out there. This brilliant, awesome idea that neither my partner nor I had considered. We went back to the agency, thought about it, worked it, made it real. Three days later, we went back and presented the new campaign. They loved it.

Creativity isn't some gene you're born with. Talent, possibly. But creativity? No. A big idea can come from anyone at any time. Not only should you believe that, but you should encourage it.

MYTH #2: THAT'S WHY THEY CALL IT WORK

So we're sitting there in Jack Connors's office on the thirty-ninth floor of the John Hancock Tower in Boston. Jack was chairman of Hill Holliday Connors and Cosmopulos, the advertising agency where I once worked as creative director for John Hancock Financial Services, Sony, Reebok, and several other clients.

The previous day, we'd presented a rough cut of a new TV spot for Starter athletic apparel to the client, and they hated it. I mean, they just despised it. So now, here we were in Jack's office facing the music. All he could say was, "Where's the joy?"

Huh? Joy? I had no idea what he was talking about.

But later, when we went back and looked at the spot again, I had to admit, Jack was right. The commercial was pretty dark. Bleak, even. Positively depressing in places. Starter was about sports and fans and the thrill of victory. Somehow we'd managed to take something that should have been fun and turned it into something somber and brooding, with defeated athletes walking off the field in the rain and slamming their helmets into lockers.

Instead of focusing on the thrill of victory, we'd chosen to go with the agony of defeat.

What about you? Do you see work as something somber and brooding? Or do you see it as something uplifting and positive and energizing and, well, joyful?

I can tell you right now, nothing smothers creativity like a company that makes you feel like you're working in a Russian gulag.

So what am I saying, that you have to leave your job and give up everything you've worked for, or turn your organization into a Chuck E. Cheese if you want to inspire your employees to think creatively? Absolutely not. Believe me, I've seen ad agencies that are so cool they could pass for some chichi art gallery in Soho. I've seen managers who wear all the latest designs and dress like they are ready for the Côte d'Azur. And I've seen other agencies that looked like the archetypal insurance company, with bosses who would wear only three-piece suits from Brooks Brothers. Guess what? A lot of the time, the agencies that looked like art galleries and the workers who looked fabulous weren't all that creative, and a lot of the ones that looked like insurance companies with workers who looked downright dowdy were bursting at the seams with great work all the time.

The mind is an inhospitable place for ideas if it thinks it's constantly under the microscope. There's a difference between play*ful* and play*ground*. Sure, maybe your employees would love it if, like Nike advertising agency Wieden+Kennedy, you put a basketball court in next to the conference room. Just like your kids would love it if you took off twelve weeks of work to take them to Disneyland. But you're probably not going to do that. And you don't have to. But if you want to see more creativity in your life or organization, you have to give people a little slack emotionally. The one thing you never want to hear in any company or family is "Where's the joy?"

> The mind is an inhospitable place for ideas, if it thinks it's constantly under the microscope.

MYTH #3: GRAPES CAN DIE ON THE VINE; SO CAN A GREAT IDEA

I really hate it when companies and people work so hard to foster creativity, when they do all the right things, say all the right things about how important ideas are to their future, only to undermine themselves by taking all eternity to implement them.

What good is a great idea if it never becomes anything more than that? Ideas don't mean much unless they can go from abstraction to reality. Otherwise, what novelist would care if his book ever got published? Maybe the architect Frank Gehry is the kind of guy who takes great satisfaction in just dreaming up his radical designs and couldn't care less if they ever actually get built. Maybe. But I doubt it.

It's always confounded me how Hollywood can be so invested in creativity and yet can so often drag a project out for years. They call this development hell, and it can last anywhere from months to decades.

The reasons are many. Maybe a screenwriter sells a script to a producer or a studio executive. They make changes. A director is brought on. He makes more changes. Maybe the star has a problem with a scene. More changes. On and on it goes until somebody just throws up their hands and says, "OK, that's it. Let's just postpone this thing." Or worse, the film gets canceled altogether.

> Ideas don't mean much unless they can go from abstraction to reality.

The William Gibson science fiction novel *Neuromancer* was optioned to be made into a film soon after the novel was published in 1984. It's been in development hell ever since. If *Neuromancer* hasn't died on the vine already, it's definitely on life support. You probably don't know that *Batman* languished for nearly ten years before it was finally made in 1989. Anne Rice sold the film rights for *Interview with the Vampire* soon after the book came out. Know how many years went by before the movie version came out? Almost twenty. No one is going to tell me that this doesn't take a terrible toll on the idea process. And anyone who thinks it doesn't obviously hasn't been to the movies in a while.

The bottom line is simply this: you can't foster a climate of personal or corporate creativity unless you're willing to greenlight those ideas for realization as quickly as possible. You can only let a person's ideas float aimlessly in space without shape or substance for so long before they dry up.

MYTH #4: DEVIL'S ADVOCATE OR IDEA ASSASSIN?

Arguably, inertia is the most powerful force in business. It's easy to get in bed with something (or someone) that works, that we trust. We get comfortable with it. And we'll resist anything that threatens that comfort level. Sometimes consciously, sometimes unconsciously.

I'm always skeptical when somebody says, "Let me just play devil's advocate."

I know you're probably wondering what's wrong with that. Not every person is perfect. Not every idea is great. Not every idea is even good. Others can seem positively brilliant in a conference room, but once they get out into the company, they can quickly reveal themselves for the unmitigated disasters that they are.

Companies should be skeptical of new ideas. People should be skeptical of new approaches to life. As we know from the New Coke debacle, ideas can be as dangerous as they can be constructive. The right idea can make you wildly successful. The wrong idea, as Coca-Cola and many other organizations can attest, has the power to maim you if not kill you. It's like plutonium. It can be good or it can be lethal. So it's OK to poke holes in people's ideas as long as your goal is to bulletproof those ideas, to find out if they leak anywhere, and to make them better. Stronger.

The problem comes when you pretend to play devil's advocate, but what you're really out to do is let your corporate baggage kill anything new. Torture it. Peck at it and peck at it and peck at it until all that's left is a few pathetic crumbs.

I can't tell you how many presentations I've been in where the client's only agenda was to kill the idea. Not because it didn't solve the problem. Not because it was off strategy. Not because it didn't capture the voice of the brand or because the tone was wrong or the copy was too hard to read. The agenda was just to kill it.

So hostile are some companies and people to anything that threatens the status quo, you could bring them the Holy Grail on a platter and they would still find something to criticize.

Bottom line? Devil's advocate, good. Trying to kill something just to kill it, bad.

MYTH #5: THE ONLY GOOD IDEA IS A BIG IDEA

We all know about the big ideas. The internal combustion engine. Sputnik. The personal computer. Television. The Internet.

These are the ideas that transcend their moment in history, whose significance slams into society like an asteroid, altering forever the cultural landscape, and that make their presence felt for decades, if not centuries.

But the world is full of small ideas, too. The little flashes of genius. The micro innovations that, while they might not shake the world, certainly have the potential to shake a small piece of it.

In their book *Ideas Are Free: How the Idea Revolution Is Liberating People and Transforming Organizations*, authors

Alan G. Robinson and Dean M. Schroeder argue that instead of expecting success to come from the big, competition-leapfrogging advances, it's the constant implementation of small ideas that ultimately wins the day.

Why is this?

Well, for one thing, it's hard to keep a home run secret. By their nature, big innovative ideas are noisy. More than noisy. Cacophonous. There's just no way around this. The really big breakthroughs get noticed and get noticed fast. Which means the odds of a competitor either copying or countering your big idea are significantly increased.

But small ideas are different.

After studying 150 companies in seventeen countries, Robinson and Schroeder concluded that small ideas tend to improve companies—and even people—in an evolutionary manner with consistent, gradual changes that are difficult if not impossible to copy, resulting in a sustainable competitive advantage.

Boardroom Inc. is a newsletter and book publisher based in Stamford, Connecticut. In 1992 Boardroom started conducting weekly department meetings. In the meetings employees are required to bring with them ideas on how to save money, new market opportunities, ways to streamline production, and anything else that might make Boardroom more profitable. Each employee is expected to average two ideas per week. To an outsider, most of the ideas might not seem like much. And while they might not be earthshaking, they've often made a difference. Like the time one Boardroom employee suggested the company cut the dimensions of its books by a quarter of an inch. Not a big idea. And yet it saved Boardroom more than $500,000 in postal costs.

It's the same in your personal life. What about saying good-bye to your husband or wife before leaving for work? What about walking to the train station in the morning instead of wasting money on gas every month? What about making less elaborate dinners every night so you could spend ten extra minutes with your family? It's the small things like these that add up to big changes in the long run.

Remember H. G. Wells's *War of the Worlds*? Remember what finally brought the aliens to their knees? It wasn't tanks or missiles or nuclear weapons or anything like that. Nope. It was the common cold. That's right. In the end, it was a microscopic germ that ended up saving the world.

Small ideas can be just as powerful.

MYTH #6: ALL I KNOW IS, IT WORKED BEFORE

Paul Simon once wrote a song about a one-trick pony. There's a lesson there for anybody who thinks that if an idea worked once, it can work again. It usually can't. So afraid are we to invent something new, to push on into unexplored creative territory, we talk ourselves into believing that a truly great idea is timeless. But is that really true? Part of what makes a great idea is that it's inextricably linked with the problem it was designed to solve. And since no two problems are exactly alike, it's pretty hard to imagine how the same idea could be anywhere near as effective when used again.

Just as you and I won't live forever, neither do ideas. Not even the best of them. Sure, the car was a big idea. But someday we're all going to move on to something else. Personal antigravity transporters. Teleportation tubes. Maybe we'll all be flying off to work with little rockets strapped to our backs. Something. And when that happens, the world will let one idea go and embrace a new one. If you've ever read *Who Moved My Cheese?*, you understand this.

You'd probably agree you can't be a successful investor if you don't know when to sell. Well, it's like that with creativity. You've got to be objective. You've got to know when an idea just isn't getting it done anymore. And you have to accept it. That's not easy. It means you have to get up off your laurels and try something new. Stick your neck out. Go where no person has gone before and all that. But what if it's different this time? What if your next idea is but a pale shadow of the big one? And if that happens, how will it change how people think of you?

Nowhere is the temptation to recycle ideas more powerful than in advertising. I once knew this woman. Really talented copywriter. Absolute superstar. The kind of person that if she had been in major league baseball would be in Cooperstown right now. Anyway, a long time ago, she came up with a campaign that went on to win every award there is in this business, and if you don't know already, there are a lot of them. Funny thing is, a year later she did another campaign for a different client. While it was different from the blockbuster work from the previous year, it wasn't really. Oh, the words were different and the visuals were different, but it was fundamentally the same idea. Same thing happened the year after that. And the thing is, none of those big idea clones were ever as successful as the real thing.

One-trick ponies might be OK in a song. But in an organization trying to foster creativity, they are a disaster.

MYTH #7: YOU CAN'T ROCK THE WORLD IF YOU DON'T ROCK THE BOAT

Risk sucks.

There's just no way around it. They might call it sticking your neck out. But it's really more like sticking your head into a pitch-black box, and you just know all kinds of flesh-eating creatures are flitting around in there, licking their chops, waiting to bite that head of yours clean off.

The more chances you take, the more you risk criticism and humiliation. It means turning your back on everything you know and facing everything you don't. Sure, you might hit it big, but you could also hit it small. Or worse.

But this much I know. Creativity cannot exist in a climate where the air is not heavy with chance. That's just a fact. Unless you're willing to accept this, innovation has about as much chance to take root in your company as a gelato stand in Newfoundland.

> If you spend all your energy trying not to fall off, how can you hope to move ahead?

It's easy to let your aversion to risk get the better of you. Sure, an idea might not pan out. Sure, it can fail. But if the occasional failure keeps you from embracing creativity at all, you'll never know what spectacular leaps forward might have happened. Pretend you're a high-wire artist in the circus. If you spend all your energy trying not to fall off, how can you hope to move ahead?

The good news is that you can embrace creativity without risking everything. Again, sometimes the best ideas are the smallest ideas. The ones that drive a company slowly and steadily forward. OK, so maybe you'll never know what it's like to grow at the speed of a starship. But the likelihood is, you'll never know what it is to crash like one either.

So go ahead and rock the boat. Rock it a little. Rock it a lot. Just rock it.

MYTH #8: WE DON'T NEED NO STINKING QUESTIONS

By now, maybe you're thinking that it's a lot easier to be creative inside the box than outside. Wrong. If anything, it's harder.

The trick is knowing precisely where the walls are, what they're made of, how thick they are, how movable or rigid they are. And the way to do that is by asking questions. "Is this wall over here really as close as it seems?" "Is that one over there really as high as I thought?" "Are the walls moving in, or are they in fact moving out?"

In her book *The Seeds of Innovation: Cultivating the Synergy That Fosters New Ideas*, Elaine Dundon argues that questions are the fuel that drives creativity. "Creative thinking begins with great questions, not answers. Great creative thinkers stay with the question instead of rushing to find an immediate solution. They ask more questions than the average person and are comfortable in the often uncomfortable situation of not immediately having the answer."

When you ask questions, you quickly discover where your real limitations lie. Especially when you ask the *right* questions.

Ask a little question, and you're likely to get a little idea, which, as we've seen in myth #5, may well be the best thing to do. Ask a big question, the kind that forces you to challenge deep assumptions that lie at the very core of your company or your soul, and you stand every chance of uncovering one of those big, quantum-leap ideas that can change the course of life.

I meant it when I said that creativity is like a nuclear reactor. Before it can unleash its energy, something really does have to get a chain reaction going. This atom splits that atom and that atom splits this atom until, whammo! Electricity happens. That's what questioning the box does. It gets a creative chain reaction going.

The problem comes when a company has spent so many years convincing itself it has *the answer* that questions are frowned upon and are not encouraged. It could be because the truth is already known and too painful to drag out from its hiding place. Or maybe people fear that if they ask the wrong questions, they'll be made to look stupid or ignorant, either to their bosses, their spouses, or themselves. It's a malignant climate that discourages creativity and, ultimately, can threaten future growth.

The Six Biggest Myths of All

Eight obstacles. Eight excuses for not allowing the inherent creativity that I know beyond any shadow of a doubt is lying there untapped in you, just waiting to be turned loose on your most challenging problems.

But as daunting as these eight barriers to creativity might seem, there are six others that I consider to be more challenging. So much so, I'm going to take on each one of them individually, in separate chapters.

But for now, here they are. The six most serious obstacles to creativity. One or all of them might well be standing between the company you are and the company I know you can be.

MYTH #9: IN LIFE, AND IN BUSINESS, NO ONE CAN HEAR YOU SCREAM

You can face the hounds of hell. You can discover an alligator in your basement. You can find a serial killer in your closet. And yet nothing can be quite so fearsome as a new idea about how to live your life or about changing your business.

The unknown is a scary thing. And for the most part, ideas are as unknown as it gets. Especially in business. Ideas don't come with a guarantee. They can and sometimes do go wrong. They can kill you quickly, or they can worm their way down deep into a company's core, infecting it with a terrible sickness that can gnaw at its insides for years.

But there is a difference between being skeptical and being terrified. Rational fear is good. Irrational fear can be debilitating. In my opinion, it's the worst barrier to creativity of them all. So much so that I've dedicated an entire chapter to it. In Chapter 4 we'll take a deeper look into the nature of creative fear and what you can do to overcome it.

MYTH #10: SO LITTLE TIME, SO FEW IDEAS

Creatively speaking, few things can constipate a company or a person like the assumption that innovation is a time-eating process. Ideas, you've been taught, take time to gestate. They can't be rushed. Unlike popcorn, you can't just stick a problem into a microwave oven and out comes a big idea a few minutes later.

If you believe this, then you are mistaken.

Popcorn can only pop inside a box. The notion that creativity and deadlines and other constraints don't mix is a complete fallacy. On the contrary, some of the most ingenious ideas in business might never have seen the light of day were it not for a ticking clock. In Chapter 5 I'm going to show you that, despite what you might believe, time is not a creativity killer but a creativity igniter.

MYTH #11: THE BIGGER THE BUDGET, THE BIGGER THE IDEA

Just as tight deadlines can be a boon to thinking creatively, so can tight budgets. You might not think so. And I would understand if you didn't. After all, ours is a culture trained to accept that no problem is insurmountable if we throw enough money at it. From big-budget movies to big-budget R&D, we've been taught that the bigger the budget, the bigger the potential idea.

We look at a big corporation with its seemingly unending flood of dollars flowing into innovation, and we wonder what chance we could possibly have with our severely limited and meager funds. We notice our next-door neighbors taking elaborate cruises and vacations and pull our hair out because we can't have as good a vacation as they do. We view these things as handicaps. But as we'll see in Chapter 6, that's true only if we perceive it that way. Once you come to understand how financial limitations can actually result in even bigger and better ideas, the true source of creativity starts to look a lot clearer and a lot more attainable.

MYTH #12: IF IT WALKS LIKE A DUCK

I'm no zoologist, but I'm pretty sure ours is the only species on the planet that lets assumptions and prejudices dictate how we live, how we think, how we arrive at decisions. It's easy to let your preconceived notions get the better of you and not bounce around inside to spur you to creativity. It's easy to let them control your ability to think beyond the status quo within the confines of your situation. But it's a definite barrier to thinking creatively. Outside the box, yes. But especially inside.

We hear a lot about profiling. But did it ever occur to you that we don't just profile people? We profile ideas. Someone has a thought, and immediately we label it. This is good. This is bad. That's smart. That's stupid. We're all opinionated. We like to think we're open-minded. But we're not. Not really. As you'll discover in Chapter 7, unless you learn to embrace your options, unless you find a way of working within them, your chances of keeping the door open to new ways of solving problems are dramatically decreased.

MYTH #13: WE HAVE OUR WAY OF DOING THINGS

I hate it when a client says, "We're too set in our ways." What is that supposed to mean? Nobody's got a gun to your head. Nobody is forcing you to stay in that rut of yours. Certainly not your employees. Not your wife or family. Not the board of directors. Nobody. The only one who benefits from preserving the status quo is the status quo. There is a difference between a rut and a box. Ruts might seem like safe places. But they're a killing field. Boxes may seem limiting. But they are the key to creativity. Pull yourself out of your rut, go into your box, and you'll amaze yourself with how creatively capable you are. Stay in your rut, and you'll slowly but surely die of inertia. And for a company or parent that isn't ready to do that, no death is more painful. We'll discuss this in detail in Chapter 8.

MYTH #14: THERE'S NO SUCH THING AS AN ORIGINAL IDEA

How many times have you heard that there are no new ideas under the sun? Well, I can't deny that. But if you think your chances of building a deeply creative life are severely compromised because of this, I will tell you right now, you are wrong.

The fact of the matter is that while there might not be any genuinely new ideas, there is an infinite supply of *com-*

binations of ideas. Was the airplane a new idea? Or was it the combination of the *idea* of a bird's wing with the *idea* of the internal combustion engine? Was a stepfamily a new idea? Or was it the combination of a traditional structure with a new twist?

In Chapter 9 we'll take a look at how it's not so much its originality that makes an idea viable as it is how well it connects seemingly unrelated concepts to create something new and wonderful.

4

It's Easy to Drown When You're Afraid of Drowning

You never feel safe when you have to navigate in waters which are completely blank.

—Lieutenant Maxwell Member,
Bering's Second Polar Expedition

I cannot imagine what it's like to put out a raging oil fire or to watch a tornado bearing down on my house or to walk out onto a ledge 127 floors above the streets of Manhattan. But I do know what it's like to sit in front of a blank computer screen trying to come up with a brilliant idea for an advertising campaign.

Knowing that I have a limited budget.

Knowing that tens of millions of dollars are at stake.

Knowing that the client happens to hate humor.

Knowing that the client's wife happens to hate humor.

Knowing that I'm going to lose the director to another project if we don't start shooting in three weeks.

Knowing that the media people are going to go into collective cardiac arrest if I come up with a sixty-second commercial when their tidy little media schedule specifically calls for thirty seconds.

Knowing that none of it's going to matter if I don't have something to present in twenty-four hours, on account of the client is going to be in Greece on vacation for the next two weeks and he either approves something before he leaves or else.

Make no mistake about it. Thinking inside the box is a lot more frightening than thinking outside the box.

I have a friend who's a photographer. Wonderful artist. Very talented. His work has hung in respected galleries all over the world. Won awards. Sold his work for tens of thousands of dollars. He is one of the most creative people I've ever known.

But there is a difference between him and me.

What I create, I create within parameters.

What he creates, he creates on his own terms. There is no client. There is no deadline. There is no bias toward black and white or color. There is only him. He either likes what he has created or he does not. I suppose you could argue that the people who buy his photographs are themselves a boundary, a clientele with likes and dislikes, and doesn't that mean he actually is creating inside a box after all? You could argue that. But trust me, that's not how it is. When this guy picks up a camera, he's shooting what appeals to *him*. Not some wealthy widow on Park Avenue. Not a corporate CEO. None of that.

As a result, he is a fearless creative person. Why? Because he can *afford* to be.

The world outside the box is a world without rules or restrictions, where you can say or think or do anything without fear of consequence.

But it's different inside the box. Unlike my friend, most of us *do* have rules and we *do* have restrictions and any attempt at creativity, by default, necessitates a confrontation with those barriers. A confrontation that we know could and, in all likelihood, will change everything. Hopefully for the better, but possibly for the worse. It can be debilitating. And it's what gives the box such power over us.

Clearly, if we're going to think creatively inside the box, we need to come to grips with the fact that (1) fear is the natural by-product of limitations and boundaries and (2) there are ways to overcome it.

With movies like *Pearl Harbor, Armageddon,* and *Con Air,* Michael Bay is one of Hollywood's most successful directors. Like David Fincher, Tarsem, and Tony Kaye, Michael Bay got his start directing TV commercials. I might be going out on a limb here, but I think that if you were to ask any of them which is more creatively challenging, a two-hour movie or a thirty-second commercial, the commercial would win hands down. Why? Because it's a whole lot more difficult to tell a compelling story in thirty seconds than it is in two or three hours. A movie gives you room to breathe. There's time to develop the characters, let the plot unfold. But a commercial is so compressed. Everything has to get boiled down. There's not a second for anything that doesn't advance the idea. It's like trying to fit the *Titanic* into a juice box. Very difficult. And if you're the one who has to pull it off, very intimidating. And yet, people like Fincher and Bay and Tarsem somehow pull it off, not because they don't feel the pressure of those thirty seconds, but because they are able to work around it.

Create Something, Destroy Something

Dr. Susan Jeffers is a psychologist and the author of *Feel the Fear and Do It Anyway*. She divides the human psyche into two parts: the Higher Self and the Chatterbox. The Higher Self is the part of us that harbors positive thoughts and positive feelings. The Chatterbox, on the other hand, is always trying to tear us down. The Higher Self says, "I'm a person with ideas, and those ideas are powerful and life altering." The Chatterbox says, "I have never had an original thought in my life, and even if I did, what good would it do because my life is what it is and nothing can ever change that, not even the most brilliant idea in the world."

Years ago I was working at a small advertising agency called Leonard Monahan Saabye in Providence, Rhode Island. Although we had only been in business for a few years, we quickly became known as one of the hottest, most award-winning young creative shops in the country. You have to understand, the advertising business is in love with awards shows. We have big national shows. We have not-so-big regional shows. We even have really small local shows.

Anyway, this particular year our agency had a lot of entries in the Hatch Awards. Hatch is a regional show held every year in Boston. I had a good feeling about my chances that year. I was confident I'd be going home with an armful of shiny silver bowls. Was I ever wrong. Oh, the agency did well all right, but all I ended up with was a long drive back to Providence feeling like my career was dead as dirt. At least, that's what my Chatterbox told me. "Man, do you suck or what. You call yourself a writer? I've seen tree sloths that can write better scripts!"

For several days after that, it went on like this until my Higher Self finally got out of the intensive care unit and back into my ear. "Hey, you. Yeah, you, whiney boy. OK, so you got skunked. Well, boo hoo. What, you think just because you didn't win a few stupid bowls, you're all of a sudden washed up? That is just stupid."

As I found out the following year, when I had a much better showing, my Higher Self was right. It *was* stupid. But I learned a lesson from that experience. Oh, sure, my Chatterbox still talks to me all the time. The difference now is that I've figured out where the mute button is. The Chatterbox, like any box, is not going away. You just have to find a way to transcend it.

When he isn't practicing microsurgery in New York City, Dr. Kenneth Kamler is practicing what he calls extreme medicine in some of the most foreboding environments on the planet. Dr. Kamler was the only physician on the ill-fated expedition up Mount Everest in 1996 made famous by Jon Krakauer in *Into Thin Air*.

In his book *Surviving the Extremes*, Dr. Kamler tells the story of his first experience as an expedition doctor. It was in Peru. Dr. Kamler and the other team members were headed toward the base of a mountain called Taqurahu. On the way, a truck filled with Indian villagers went off the road, plunging down into a ravine. The Andes Mountains weren't New York City. There were no ambulances. No world-class emergency rooms mere blocks away. No emergency rooms, period. And yet, moments later, Dr. Kamler had moved beyond his initial fear and was down in the ravine, moving from victim to victim, setting broken arms, starting intravenous lines, treating concussions. "Gradually, it became clear that although I was high up in the Andes, I was facing injuries not unlike those I would find in any hospital's emergency room."

Did Dr. Kamler feel fear? Of course he did. Did he have the high-tech machines and materials he was used to working with? No. He was forced to think inside the box and deal with what he had. Unlike many of us, he had the ability to move from feeling the fear to confronting it to surmounting it.

Creativity, by its very nature, is a destructive act in the sense that to give birth to something new inherently requires the death of something old. Creativity, after all, is about change. And change is never easy. We might *think* we want change. But at the same time, we're afraid of it.

Why is that? Because it means moving out of our comfort zone.

This is an important concept to understand.

Think of the comfort zone you're in right now as a room. There's another room next door. That's a comfort zone, too. Not yours, maybe, but someone's. Maybe you can envision yourself in that room. Maybe you can imagine what it would be like to be in that room. "If only I could be there instead of here," you think, "things would be better. If only this damn wall weren't in the way. If only I weren't so damn afraid."

> Creativity, after all, is about change. And change is never easy.

My wife is a newspaper columnist. But a long time ago, she was an advertising account executive. One day she went to work and found out that she no longer had a job. This might not have been a problem in a big city like New York or Los Angeles, where it can seem like there's an advertising agency on every corner. But this was Providence, Rhode Island. You could literally count the jobs in advertising on the head of a pin, and a very small pin at that.

There was another problem. At the time, she was a divorced single mother with a five-year-old son and only three, maybe four months of savings to tide her over. After that she was going to be in serious trouble. If you've ever looked down the barrel of this particular gun, you know that the thought of your money running out can scare you senseless.

Even so, she knew that if she could only get on the other side of the thing, life could actually be better. The fact was, she'd grown increasingly frustrated in her old job. Although her performance reviews had consistently been outstanding and her clients were enthusiastic about her, other employees in the company who weren't carrying nearly her workload were making a lot more money. So in one sense, her employers had done her a favor. But in another sense, they'd strapped her to a ticking financial bomb. This was her box.

And then something happened. At the height of her panic, she had an idea. Maybe she could start a new kind of advertising agency. But how? Like any start-up, it takes money to get a new ad agency off the ground. The really good people in the business do not come cheap, and that is just their salaries, to say nothing of benefits packages. With barely enough savings left to pay her mortgage, she knew she had no business even thinking about something like this let alone actually going through with it.

But she also knew that not all the best people in advertising worked for companies, preferring to freelance. She thought, "Instead of having a permanent staff with all of its attendant payroll and benefits, why not do it the way Hollywood makes movies?" Depending on the film, the production company assembles a handpicked team—director, director of photography, actors, lighting experts, sound people, and hundreds of others—to do the project. Why couldn't the same model work for advertising?

Couldn't you simply outsource all the most vital job functions to freelance writers, art directors, and media buyers on a project-by-project basis? It was exactly the same model that Hollywood used. And if it could work for making a movie, why couldn't it work for making an advertising campaign?

As it turns out, it did.

She went through with her idea, and it turned out to be very successful. Since then a number of other agencies have adopted the same Hollywood model, and it's worked equally well for them. She looked around at the confines of her box (money, being a single parent, etc.) and made it work for her.

What Would Franklin D. Roosevelt Have Done?

A long time ago, FDR told us that the only thing we had to fear was fear itself. And that goes as much for creativity as for facing a Depression or fighting a World War. Nothing can freeze your creative self in its tracks like fear. Ask any writer. It's amazing how a blank computer screen can put the fear of God into even the most talented of authors. And yet somehow they find a way to short-circuit that fear.

A moment ago, I said that a ticking financial bomb can scare you senseless. And it definitely can. But as my wife demonstrated, it can also scare you into new realms of creativity. The trick is to compartmentalize. No one is saying you have to conquer your fear. But you do have to be able to contain it. There has to be a way of allowing yourself to feel it and yet do what needs to be done in spite of what you're feeling.

> No one is saying you have to conquer your fear. But you do have to be able to contain it.

Most people who know me personally know that I stutter. For nearly my entire life, it's been a source of perpetual frustration to me. Especially when I was a kid. In school I lived in mortal fear of being called on. I knew there was no such thing as making yourself invisible, but believe me, if I could have, I would have. I tried to avoid any and all occasions in which I might have to actually stand up in front of a classroom and say something. It was horrible.

I remember when I was a sophomore in high school. Physics class. We all had to give an oral report on our science projects. Let me just say this—I would have happily stuck needles in my eyes, had it meant getting out of that assignment.

It wasn't like I hadn't been through this before. And every time, I would stammer and choke and gag in a desperate but pathetic attempt to speak. If I managed to spit out three words a minute, I was doing well. Like I said, it was horrible.

So much did I fear the thought of humiliating myself yet again in front of my classmates that when the day for my report finally came around, I decided there was just no way I was going to go through with it. So naturally instead of going to school that morning, I took a detour to the local movie theater, where I spent the day watching Vincent Price in *The Pit and the Pendulum* over and over until it was time to go home.

This was, of course, stupid. Needless to say, I had only given myself a stay of execution, because the very next day I had to show up in class and do the report anyway.

Interestingly, there was another kid in my class who also had a speech impediment. But where I was always trying to hide the problem, run away from it, Russell Lollicata didn't do that. On the contrary, while I was hiding behind the kid in front of me, Russell actually raised his hand to answer questions! That day I was doing my little Vincent Price marathon, Russell was getting an A on his oral report. I admired his courage. As Russell and I went through high school, I also noticed that his speech seemed to be getting better, while mine wasn't. Russell had accepted the limitations of his box, embraced them, and moved on from there.

I ran into Russell at my tenth high school reunion. He made a speech that night, and I was very impressed. He had no sign of a stutter at all. Not a trace. Later I told him how much I'd envied the fact that he'd never been afraid to speak up in class. Know what he said? "What the hell are you talking about? I was petrified." Where I had let my fear of embarrassing myself stop me from participating in class, Russell just did it. And the more he did it, the better he got at it.

Dan Osman was one of the most famous rock climbers in the world. He believed that the only way to get past your fear of falling was falling. That you cannot fully calm your fear of falling until you actually experience what it's like to lose your grip on the rock, see the ground rushing up at you, and ultimately feel the tug of your safety harness as the rope stops you from plunging to your death. He, too, knew that embracing your box was the only way to get better at what you do, either personally or professionally.

"The best way out is always through." Helen Keller said that. She was right.

The Five Biggest Fears That Keep You from Being Creative

While there are as many reasons for people to be afraid of letting their imaginations wander off into unexplored territory as there are people, there are five that are responsible for more failures to innovate than all the rest.

FEAR OF FAILING

People don't like to make fools of themselves. I certainly didn't when I was a kid trying, in vain, to hide my stutter. The question you have to ask is, "What's the worst that can happen?" This is an important question. The reason is that the answer almost always is, "Not much."

> If you've got an idea and you're afraid someone is going to think poorly of it, go for it anyway.

It's true. If we're talking about a nuclear power plant going China Syndrome, then sure, the worst that can happen is pretty bad. But if we're talking about an idea that might improve how your department can enhance productivity or how your children's school could raise more money for a new playground, then the worst that can happen is, what, a patronizing smile? A polite brush-off? The point is, if you've got an idea and you're afraid someone is going to think poorly of it, go for it anyway. Embrace what you have and get your ideas out there. Who knows, maybe people will think you're a genius.

FEAR OF SUCCEEDING

It sounds weird when you put it that way. But trust me, it happens all the time. Whether we're willing to admit it or not, some of us don't really want to have a creative thought, because it might actually work. We may have generated an idea within our own boxes, and if it actually works, we might get noticed. And if we get noticed, people might raise their expectations about us. And if they raise their expectations, we might have to come up with another creative idea and, God forbid, maybe another and another after that. Worse yet, each succeeding idea will have to be bigger and better than the one before it. But that just isn't true. In advertising nobody has great ideas all the time. Ideas, yes. That's what we get paid for. But bigger and better, time after time? Doesn't happen. If it did, TiVo would still be nothing but a twinkle in its inventor's eye. Marianne Williamson once wrote, "Our deepest fear is not that we are inadequate. Our deepest fear is that we are powerful beyond measure." Ideas are powerful things. They're meant to do wonderful things. Don't be afraid of them.

FEAR OF CHANGE

Creativity is the displacement of one idea or one way of doing things with something new and hopefully better. But is better always better? Will our new box be better than our old box? Will it make us any happier? Maybe the rut we're in isn't great, but at least it's our rut and we've gotten pretty damn comfortable here. Do we really want to risk changing that? Understand, you are not the first who has asked these questions, and you will not be the last. As human beings, we might *say* we want to change the status quo. But deep down, not many of us actually want to succeed. Change means leaving behind the known for the unknown. And the unknown is, has always been, and shall always be a pretty dark and shadowy place. Until you get there. Once you do, you realize just how much better the new way is over the old way. This is almost always true. And in those rare cases when it isn't—well, what's stopping you from going back? I knew a guy who struggled for years to sell a screenplay to Hollywood. Guess what happened when he finally succeeded? That's right. He hated it. Hated L.A. Hated the business. Hated the parties. Hated everything about it. First chance he got, he was back in Boston at his old, unglamorous job as marketing director for a big athletic shoe company.

FEAR OF GOING BROKE

While it doesn't take much money to write a novel or paint or sculpt, there are times when being creative necessarily means more than just an investment of your time. Maybe a lot more. Maybe you've got a brilliant invention swimming around in your head. Maybe a business that no one's ever tried before. These are the kinds of creative ideas that, until you are willing to invest money in them, will never be more than just ideas. But are there ways to minimize the risk? How can you think inside the constraints of your limiting, financial box? Maybe you can borrow money from a friend or relative. Maybe you cut back on expenses to help fund the idea. Do you really need to go to the movies every week? Could you drive a less luxurious car? In other words, are you willing to make a sacrifice or two to turn your idea into something real that could come back to benefit you many times over? Yeah, it's a gamble. But it's a gamble on yourself. And if you're not worth it, nobody is.

FEAR OF TIME

Like anything else, creativity rarely happens in the blink of an eye. It takes time. It takes time to ponder a problem. To let it gestate in your mind. To think. The problem is, what if we don't have enough time to pursue our ideas? It's hard enough juggling all the things in our lives. Our jobs. Our kids. Our relationships. Who can possibly find the time to imagine anything new? I'll tell you who can. You can.

Sometimes, time constraints generate the best ideas. You know how I know this? Because other people as busy and maybe busier than you have done exactly that. Before John Grisham became a bestselling novelist, he was John Grisham the lawyer and state legislator. Attorneys are not known for their vast pockets of free time, let alone attorneys who also happen to be state legislators. Technically, Grisham did not have time to write *A Time to Kill*. But, of course, he did. How? By forcing himself to get up at two o'clock in the morning and write until he had to get ready for work. He might not have *had* the time, but he sure did manage to *find* it anyway. Had he not had those time constraints, he might not be the immensely successful author he is today. Grisham found the time, and so can you.

While your son is at hockey practice, could you work on your idea? While you're on the train going home from work at night, instead of chatting with the guy next to you, might that time be better spent doing a little personal brainstorming? Do you really have to watch that reality show on TV every week, or could you invest an extra hour in changing your own reality? Seriously. You think the time isn't there. It's there. It's just occupied at the moment with something else.

5

He's Been in There for Three Minutes!

The Power of Deadlines

A deadline is negative inspiration.
Still, it's better than no inspiration
at all.

—RITA MAE BROWN

In August of 2002, T. M. Amabile, C. N. Hadley, and S. J. Kramer published an article in the *Harvard Business Review* that basically confirmed what creative people have been saying ever since the first artist started scribbling crude drawings of woolly mammoths on the walls of his cave.

The authors collected and analyzed more than 9,000 daily e-mail diary entries from 177 professional employees from seven companies in the chemical, high-tech, and consumer products industries. Each was involved in projects where creativity was crucial to the project's success. The sample was relatively substantial in size, with a response rate of 75 percent and all 177 professionals participating for longer than six months

When the results finally came in, the authors concluded that, although there are exceptions, when creativity is under the gun, it usually ends up getting shot dead.

Because the study was and still is well respected, its impact has become widespread, with hundreds of references to it on the Internet alone. If companies faced with the reality of tighter and tighter deadlines thought they couldn't be creative before because they didn't have the time, now they were certain of it. And that's unfortunate. While Amabile, Hadley, and Kramer are right in saying that creativity can suffer once the fuse starts burning, it's by no means a foregone conclusion.

Like everyone else in advertising, I've had to innovate within the box of time for my entire career. It's just the way it is in this business. I can count on one hand the number of times I've had the luxury of having longer than a month to work on a project. Did I say month? In a lot of cases, you're lucky to get two, maybe three weeks. And usually we're talking a matter of days. Even hours.

In 1985 Ammirati & Puris was one of the hottest advertising agencies in America. Among their clients were BMW, Schweppes, Club Med, and the Four Seasons. The agency had won widespread acclaim for its groundbreaking work. After winning an assignment from United Parcel Service, Ammirati was eager to show what it could do with the launch of the company's move into overnight shipping, where it would go toe-to-toe with Federal Express. From the outset UPS had made it clear that under no circumstances did it want to so much as acknowledge the existence of FedEx. Nor did it want to say that UPS was two-thirds less expensive than FedEx.

For weeks the agency struggled. The client wanted to take the high ground. But the creative people didn't know where to go with this, feeling intuitively that the imposed creative restriction was needless and a mistake. UPS had a blatant advantage over FedEx. Why would UPS not want the world to know that?

Mark Silveira and Mark Moffett were one of the creative teams who'd been brought in to try and break the logjam. "Everybody was struggling with the higher ground thing," Silveira said. "We were all creatively stuck. Moffett and I were leaving for a shoot in Paris in a couple of days. We figured what the hell and just went ahead and did some stuff that went right after FedEx."

Not surprisingly, the ideas were shot down by agency management just as Silveira and Moffett assumed that they would be. But the work did get the agency asking questions about UPS that it hadn't asked before. "We figured that the reason UPS could equal FedEx's service at a lower price was because UPS was such a fanatical company about wringing every last drop of efficiency out of its operation." It was an insight that led another Ammirati copywriter to create the line "We run the tightest ship in the shipping business."

With the presentation to UPS scheduled for the next morning, the teams went back and furiously set to work developing new commercials. But when they finally presented the creative that night, yet another problem emerged. As Ammirati president Ed Vick was quick to point out, there weren't any airplanes in the spots. Not a single one. Yes, the new commercials were on strategy. Yes, they were creative. Yes, they'd probably be extremely effective. But there weren't any planes. And without planes, Vick felt, UPS would never go for it.

With twelve hours remaining until the presentation, the agency creative people went back to work. They had a strategy. They had a great tagline. And a clock that was ticking. Loudly. All through that night, everyone focused on airplane spots. Nobody went anywhere. Nobody slept. Nobody went out for dinner. Nobody took a shower. Nobody thought about anything except packages, overnight deliveries, tight ships, and, of course, airplanes. They were stuck in their box, and they pulled it out.

At ten o'clock the next morning, the Ammirati & Puris team presented the new advertising to UPS at the company's headquarters in Greenwich, Connecticut. To say the presentation was a success is putting it mildly. The campaign was enthusiastically received by UPS management and went on to be enormously successful. "It was a matter of intense focus," says Silveira. "That, combined with the fact that there was no time to think, let alone overthink."

I can tell you this much. In advertising, the Ammirati & Puris story is not an exceptional one. There isn't a copywriter or an art director in the world who hasn't spent many a long, sleepless night scrambling to dream up an incredibly creative campaign in a matter of hours.

But it isn't just advertising where short fuses have resulted in big ideas. Dr. Andrei Linde is a professor of physics at Stanford University. He is widely regarded as one of the leading theoretical physicists in the world. In 1986, while still a citizen of the former Soviet Union, Dr. Linde suffered a crippling depression. Like John Nash, the Nobel Prize–winning mathematician made famous by the movie *A Beautiful Mind*, whose life and career were also derailed for a time by mental illness, Andrei Linde could barely get out of bed, let alone engage in complicated thoughts involving the nature of the universe. But with a prestigious conference in Italy looming and one of its most celebrated scientists scheduled to speak there, the Kremlin was unsympathetic. Linde would make the speech and he would introduce a brilliant new theorem while doing so, or else—well, I think we know what else. Despite both his depression and the irrationally intense time pressure, Linde managed to come up with his self-replicating universe theory. But here's the really amazing part. He did it in thirty minutes. And his ideas are now one of the cornerstones of science.

And then there's Cinemasports.

Like Austin, Sundance, Park City, and dozens of other cities around the country, Santa Cruz is widely regarded as an artistic city with more than a passing interest in music, dance, and film. Since its founding, the Santa Cruz Film Festival has typically attracted a large and enthusiastic crowd drawn to the innovative and often experimental movies made by little-known filmmakers. Many are there to win an award. Most are hoping they'll get noticed by one of the major studios or production companies. The 2005 festival was no different. Among the films fans saw that year were *The Real Dirt on Farmer John*, *High Ambitions*, *Commune*, and *Imagining Ulysses*. All were excellent movies, and all played well with both critics and audiences.

But it was a series of short films made under less-than-ideal conditions that got much of the attention. Like "The Iron Chef," a popular reality cooking TV show, Cinemasports is a unique experience in moviemaking, a competition in which small teams of contestants, armed with a digital camera and a short list of must-have shots, have nine hours to come up with an idea, shoot it, edit it, and screen it that same evening. Needless to say, nine hours is an incredibly short amount of time to even conceive an idea for a film, let alone actually see that idea through to completion. But then add to that the fact that the film has to include, say, a three-legged cat, a man eating oranges, a suit of armor, a sombrero, and a jockey wearing nothing but a lime green jockstrap, and you can see the difficulty. And yet the results are often impressive, with audiences consistently praising the films for their creativity and unencumbered moviemaking genius. Sometimes being under the gun can allow you to think more creatively than ever.

This crosses over into people's personal lives. Take the story of Liam, who was an excellent student in college. He had consistently gotten As on all of his papers but had somehow let the deadline for one paper, on Shakespeare's *King Lear*, get the better of him. He had twelve hours to come up with a topic, research it, and write a paper on it. The result? The first A+ paper of his college career.

Tom Monahan is the president of Before and After, one of the most highly regarded creative training companies in the world. He's worked with leading corporations like ABC, Hasbro, and the Wall Street Journal, and neither Andrei Linde's experience or that of Cinemasports surprises him. "The good news about thinking fast is that, by definition, it means you're taking judgment out of it," Monahan says. "Fully half the people I work with tell me they work better under pressure. To those who say they don't, you were born in the wrong century. Things move much faster today than ever before, and obviously the race goes to the swift."

Does it ever.

When he was still CEO of General Electric, Jack Welsh had this to say: "My job today is ten times faster than it was five years ago. A hundred times. The pace is enormously quicker because of technology. So everyone has to gear themselves to a faster pace, to more competitiveness, to more intellectual capital. That's the game." Speed was a huge deal for Welsh. During his tenure, GE Appliances announced a new product every ninety days. A General Electric jet engine was designed and manufactured in half the normal time. The company also conceived, developed, and built a new locomotive in what, at the time at least, was a mind-numbingly torrid pace. From concept to market in just eighteen months.

But if Welsh thought business and life were running fast in the 1990s, they're positively moving at the speed of light now. And they aren't about to slow down anytime soon. In a marketplace that's moving faster every day, in a world where fathers and mothers have to career between soccer practice, tutors, school plays, and dance lessons, speed is gold. It doesn't matter how big you are. It doesn't matter how powerful you are. It doesn't matter how smart you are. Unless you can accomplish big things in a compressed amount of time, you are in deep trouble. Contrary to what you might have learned from the Rolling Stones, time is not on your side. Not that it ever was. But it's worse now. Suddenly, years have become months. Months have become weeks. Weeks have become days. In every sense, you are in a race. To get to market first. To get to the grocery store before it closes. To outflank competitors. To jog a few miles before the 7:54 train leaves. To build strategic alliances.

> Unless you can accomplish big things in a compressed amount of time, you are in deep trouble.

And yet there are those who will tell you that creativity cannot function in a climate like this. Creativity, they tell us, is like a rare orchid that can only flourish with perfect humidity, perfect sunlight, perfect temperatures. Ideas, they will tell you, cannot be rushed. They have to be watered and fed. They have to be allowed to incubate and ferment, and when they're ready, they'll be ready and not a moment sooner. In their opinion, epiphanies are the children of time. And lots of it.

Are they wrong? In an ideal world, no. But that's just the problem. There's simply no such thing. Not in this universe anyway. Certainly not for companies rushing into the future at a million miles an hour or for mothers juggling two children while holding down a full-time job. Tell Mark Silveira about fermenting. Tell Tom Monahan about incubating.

Sure, it sounds good. But unless you're in business to amuse yourself—and I'm going to stick my neck out here and assume you're not—you learn to create under the gun or you don't create at all. And in today's innovation-driven economy, that's just not an option.

So what's the answer? How can you prepare your company to think creatively even under the worst of time crunches? What can you do to encourage innovative thinking even with the sound of a clock ticking like a jackhammer in your ears? There are five things you can do.

1. Why Do You Think They Call It a Surgical Strike?

On June 27, 1976, Air France flight AF139 en route from Tel Aviv to Paris was hijacked by four terrorists. The plane, on which nearly one-third of the passengers were Israelis, was flown to Benghazi. After a six and a half hour delay, the plane took off again. By three o'clock the next morning, it had landed at Entebbe Airport in Uganda.

By Friday, July 2, Israel already had created a plan of attack. Less than twenty-four hours later, three C-130 Hercules transport planes that had been painted to look like Ugandan jets began the long flight from Israel to Entebbe with more than two hundred elite commandos aboard. Surprising both the Ugandan troops guarding the hostages and the terrorists, the commandos attacked. Within an hour, the remaining hostages and crew were safe and on their way back to Israel.

The Entebbe raid is considered one of the most successful surgical strikes ever mounted. Why? Because the team was given a single-minded mission: get the hostages out of Entebbe, and fast. The hijackers had made their demands and had vowed to start shooting the hostages. The time pressure had to have been stupefying. A laser beam could not have been more sharply focused. There were no changes in the objective. No politicians weighing in. No squabbles within the chain of command.

In advertising we have something called a creative brief. Basically, it's just a short document with all the information that's pertinent to a given project. Who is the audience? What are the psychographics? Where is the ad going to run? What's the background information? Who is the competition? All of it important stuff to know. But I might as well be honest. There's really just one thing the creative team is interested in: what is the single-minded point we need to make?

Let me repeat that.

What is the single-minded point we need to make?

You'll notice I said *single*-minded. Not *double*-minded or *triple*-minded. Single-minded. What is the one thing about this project that the client wants to sell to the world? Though it sounds easy enough, I cannot tell you the number of times I've had to fight hammer and tong with some clients over this. But there's too much to say, they've told me. How can we possibly boil it all down to one simple sentence? And then I remind them about the raid on Entebbe: *get the hostages out.*

> What is the single-minded point we need to make?

Stavros Cosmopulos had a different way of making the same point. Literally. Stavros was one of the founding partners of the advertising agency Hill Holliday Connors and Cosmopulos in Boston. Whenever a client would chafe at the idea of focusing on one message in an ad, he'd bring out two pieces of plywood. One had dozens of nails sticking up out of it. The other one had a single nail. He'd lay both boards down on the conference room table, and he'd say to the client, "If I asked you to take off your shoes and stand on one of these, which one do you think you'd be more likely to remember?"

It's amazing the ideas that people can come up with, even against the worst of deadlines, when they have a clear sense of mission. That means one simple objective. Repeat after me. One. Simple. Objective.

2. Put the Blinders On

I don't know much about racehorses. But I do know that some animals tend to get more distracted than others. You can have a horse that's incredibly fast, though just the mere sight of other horses, a sudden movement in the infield, or a truck rumbling along a nearby highway can be enough to spook the daylights out of him. But put a pair of blinders on his head, keep him focused on the track, keep him zeroed in on the finish line and watch him go.

When time isn't a factor, distractions can be great for creativity. It's no coincidence that most advertising agencies have plenty of them: pool tables, pachinko machines, dart boards, Nerf Frisbees, jukeboxes. If you've never been in an agency creative department, it can seem more like a playground than a business office. I know one place that brings in bands on Friday afternoons and another that has a full-blown basketball court in the basement. This is a good thing. Under ideal circumstances, play and creativity are two sides of the same coin.

Until all hell breaks loose.

Once the countdown starts, distractions are the kiss of death. Suddenly, anything and everything that isn't relevant to the project is a potential focus breaker and therefore a full-tilt creativity assassin.

> Under ideal circumstances, play and creativity are two sides of the same coin. Until all hell breaks loose.

As reported by the BBC News World Edition, a recent study conducted for Hewlett-Packard found that workers distracted by e-mail, phone calls, and text messaging suffer an average ten-point drop in IQ, more than twice as bad as commonly results from smoking marijuana. The effect on creativity can be even worse. If you want to maximize the odds of big ideas happening in very compressed time periods, make sure everyone on the project understands the rules. Unplug the Ethernet cables. Turn off the cell phones. Check the Blackberrys at the door.

And speaking of distractions, try to keep a lid on meetings. Nothing can suck away creative time faster than unnecessary meetings. Particularly if they aren't relevant. And sometimes even if they are. Obviously, meetings that waste time are only going to make the time pressure worse. If they're absolutely necessary though, keep them short, tight, and nonjudgmental. Get to the point. Make it. Shut up. Move on. Unless they've got something to do with the project, the words *weather, weekend, sports, movies,* and *vacation,* to name but a few, should not come up.

The same holds true if you are trying to get home to your family. A coworker may try to engage you in idle chitchat or might want to talk about last night's game. Accept the box that you have to get home by six o'clock, put your blinders on, and firmly tell her that you have to go.

Understand that what might be a distraction to me might be a necessary part of the creative thought process to you. Personally, unlike my kids, who seem to do a much better job getting their homework done with, say, Gwen Stefani blaring in their iPod earbuds, I can't work with music on. A personal quirk that author Stephen King obviously doesn't share with me. King routinely listens to heavy metal bands like AC/DC and Metallica when he's writing. Likewise for fellow horror novelist Charles L. Grant, although Grant prefers movie sound tracks. So there are exceptions. But make sure they're legitimate ones. Otherwise, dump them.

3. Jeff Gordon? Yes. Kyle Busch? No.

After four lead changes in the last nine laps, racing legend Jeff Gordon came from behind to win the 2005 Daytona 500.

Kyle Busch did not. Kyle Busch was a rookie. He'd never driven in the Daytona 500 before. Was he a good driver? Sure, at least compared to you or me. But he was nowhere near as good as Gordon. At least not at Daytona. Why not?

Sure, his car probably wasn't as fast as Gordon's. Fast cars cost money. A lot of it. A luxury not usually afforded to rookies. For the same reason, Busch's pit crew probably wasn't as fast as Gordon's either. There could have been other reasons. Bad luck. Bad karma. But there's a bigger reason why Jeff Gordon won and Kyle Busch didn't.

Gordon was experienced.

Busch wasn't.

I don't care how bright they are. I don't care if they've got the work ethic of a Clydesdale. I don't care if they got their MBA from Harvard or Babson or Carnegie Mellon. If inexperienced people are thrown against a flaming hot project, if they are put in the box of pressure, there's an excellent chance they're going to go the way of Kyle Busch.

What am I saying, that inexperienced people aren't creative? No. Under sane conditions, they might well be as creative as anyone else in the company. Maybe more so. But this isn't about sane conditions. This is about insane conditions, when hellfire is raining down and the wheels are threatening to fall off. This is when you need people with the unique ability to self-edit themselves and to accept the confines of their boxes and who can then make instantaneous creative assessments. Is the idea good or is it bad? Is it worth expanding or do you leave it behind?

4. Three Hundred Stealth Fighters Can't Be Wrong

For years Lockheed Martin operated a little-known organization out in the Nevada desert. Cloaked in mystery, the Skunk Works was an extraordinarily creative engine that turned out some of this country's most technologically advanced aircraft, often so much so that they were consistently mistaken for UFOs in the early stages of testing.

Kelly Johnson, one of the driving forces at the Skunk Works, would probably tell you that one of the biggest reasons it succeeded was the limited number of people involved in any given project. If you were to compare the number of people involved with the creation of the F-117 stealth fighter or the SR-71 supersonic spy plane with, say, the creation of the Boeing 777 passenger liner, it would be no contest. Because the Skunk Works teams are smaller, they're more efficient, more nimble, and less prone to meddling. This is a classic example of a company that accepted the limitations of the number of people it was able to afford and used that box to be more creative than its competitors.

It's the same with families. Which are the more pleasant gatherings: a quiet night at home with your nearest and dearest or a loud raucous evening when Aunt Mildred won't sit next to Uncle Joe, and your niece Evelyn gets into a conversation with your wife?

I wish I could tell you that advertising agencies and the Skunk Works have a lot in common. But I can't. Unfortunately, as good as Madison Avenue is at coping with crushing creative deadlines in every other respect, keeping a lid on the number of people involved with a project is not something advertising normally embraces. To the contrary, the temptation is to bring in as many people as possible in the hope that somebody will stumble over a brilliant, groundbreaking solution. Creative directors will tell you that this is smart. That the odds of nailing that brilliant solution are a lot better if you're throwing a battalion against the problem than if you're throwing a platoon. And that is true. But so are the chances for agendas.

In 1981 Pat Fallon, Tom McElligott, and Nancy Rice opened for business in downtown Minneapolis. By all measures their fledgling shop should have remained a small regional advertising agency with small regional clients. But with its edgy, smart, creative work, the tiny agency quickly made a name for itself, going on to win hundreds of national awards. Fallon McElligott Rice didn't win those accounts by beating up on agencies its own size. In fact, they often did it by competing and winning against some of the biggest agencies on Madison Avenue. Like its competitors, Fallon McElligott Rice sometimes had the luxury of having sufficient time to prepare for a new business pitch. Many times it didn't. If the big agency mentality is correct, that the more brains you throw at a project, the better your chances of success, then you would think a small agency like Fallon McElligott Rice would have been at a huge disadvantage. It was, after all, a much smaller company with nowhere near the creative resources. Not even close. And yet time and again, the upstart Minneapolis shop managed to knock off its bigger competitors. Why? Because it had a tight Skunk Works–type team with enormous talent and a keen sense of mission. It was nimble. It was focused. It was single-minded. It was driven and efficient and undistracted by competing egos. Fallon McElligott Rice embraced the box of its small size and worked it to their advantage. It's not about having

> It's not about having a lot of brains working on a project. It's about having the right brains.

a lot of brains working on a project. It's about having the right brains. Once that fuse starts burning, I'll take my chances with a small team of supremely talented people any day.

5. Just Because Stephen King Would Buy It Doesn't Mean Stephen Hawking Would

When time isn't a factor, people can afford to make mistakes creatively. So what if an idea, as great as it is, turns out to be impossible to implement. There's still plenty of time to keep thinking. Who knows? If it's a really big idea, maybe changes can be made to accommodate it.

But when time *is* a factor, you have no such luxury. Under-the-gun ideas have got to work right out of the box. If an idea can't be implemented, and quickly, then for all intents and purposes, it isn't really an idea at all.

> Under-the-gun ideas have got to work right out of the box.

For this reason, it's important that even the tightest, leanest creative Skunk Works team include a left-brain thinker. Someone whose sole purpose is to ask questions, poking holes in arguments and making ideas run the gauntlet of practicality.

Is this really necessary? I believe it is, and here's why.

Advertising creative people tend to be a pretty intuitive bunch. The best ones have a kind of sixth sense that tells them which ideas will touch people, reach them in places that other ideas wouldn't. Apple's "1984," arguably the most influential TV commercial ever made, was roundly rejected by Apple's board of directors. But Chiat/Day (Apple's advertising agency), convinced the spot was a winner, fought for the idea and ultimately aired the ninety-second commercial in the third quarter of the 1984 Super Bowl, where it quickly gained near-mythical status. Could Chiat/Day prove the spot would work? Not at all. But they *felt* it. And they were right. Was "1984" a fluke? Not really. Advertising creative people routinely come up with extraordinarily effective ideas that have defied the protestations of every critic from board chairmen to focus group attendees.

But it doesn't work all the time. I've seen just as many brilliant campaigns fall flat on their face. Campaigns that the creative team swore up and down and six ways to Sunday would exceed every expectation.

The thing to remember is, if you want people to be free to think creatively, it's OK to trust their intuitive abilities to a point. And you want to nurture that. But intuition isn't always bulletproof. So do yourself a favor and put a left-brain thinker on the team. Tell this person to bring plenty of bullets—and not be afraid to use them.

Bottom line? Time doesn't have to be the stifling obstacle that some people make it out to be, if you know how to manage it properly. So define your single-minded mission. Be ruthless about minimizing distractions. Trust experience. Keep the team lean and tight. Shoot holes in everything. And above all, start seeing the deadlines in your life as a positive force that can energize your thinking. What would rivers be without riverbanks? They wouldn't be rivers at all. They'd be a shapeless mass of water that's going everywhere and therefore nowhere. Time limits are like riverbanks. Be thankful for them.

Creativity and the Straitjacket of Money

> *Lack of money is no obstacle. Lack of an idea is an obstacle.*
>
> —KEN HAKUTA, TOY INVENTOR

If I were to take you to Cohen Alley, a seedy dead end in San Francisco's Tenderloin district, I doubt you'd consider it a hotbed of creative thinking.

On any given night, it's common to encounter everything from pimps and prostitutes to strung-out crack dealers on most street corners. You won't find it on any tourist map, and if you happen to live in San Francisco, you'd probably be hard-pressed to find a reason to go anywhere near the place.

Everywhere you look, there's scary stuff. If it isn't the porn shops, it's the wail of police car sirens. It's a rough neighborhood.

And yet every weekend for six months in 2003, some of the most talented photographers in the city would set up their cameras in Cohen Alley, offering to take pictures of any of the hundreds of homeless people who live in the area.

If I asked you to look at those same people and tell me what you see, you probably wouldn't see much to photograph. These are homeless people after all. Not exactly the same as shooting pictures of redwood trees or fashion models or Thoroughbred horses. There's not much beauty in homelessness. This is what you'd probably think.

Where most of us couldn't get past the tattered clothing, the stubbly beards, the plastic trash bags overflowing with personal belongings, these photographers saw something vastly different—a sharp and chiseled grace, a gritty attractiveness that most people never see. Unless they happen to be homeless themselves.

The Sixth Street Photography Workshop (SSPW) was founded in 1991 by Tom Ferentz, a professional photographer and the group's artistic director. Its mission is to share the art and skills of photography with homeless and low-income adults and young people. SSPW recruits the fledgling artists from local shelters, residential hotels, social service agencies, and community organizations. They are supplied with film, paper, and cameras and have access to the group's darkroom and studio facilities. If the students are interested in going further, they're invited to move into an advanced program where they learn to conceptualize projects, take photographs, print images, and mount exhibits. More than three hundred people have gone through the program, some for as long as ten years.

With its haunting and starkly beautiful photographic portraits and personal narratives of San Francisco's homeless, SSPW's Stories of the City is an incredible exhibition. It documents the lives of San Francisco's poor in a way that I've seldom seen. It's powerful and incredibly moving. I've seen a lot of photography, and I can tell you that Stories of the City is unbelievably compelling work.

The exhibit explores the gamut of homelessness, from cultural identity, ethnicity, work, and unemployment to drugs, recovery, hope, love, and family. The photographs tell a poignant story of a life as alien to most of us as the surface of Mars, one that we cannot begin to truly imagine. They're extraordinary.

You look at this work, and it's easy to think of critically acclaimed artists like Steve McCurry or Annie Leibovitz, deservedly world-famous photographers with elaborate studios, expensive cameras, an arsenal of lenses, the latest lighting systems, and spectacularly equipped darkrooms. But then you realize that these incredible pictures were taken by homeless people. Their cameras weren't the most expensive. Neither was the lighting equipment. They worked in a borrowed darkroom. They didn't have paid assistants. And yet the photographs are so engaging, so gripping in their ability to connect with us, it doesn't seem possible. How could anything so creative be accomplished with so little?

It's easy to think that big ideas and big budgets are synonymous. But it's far from the truth.

In his excellent book, *Hey, Whipple, Squeeze This*, advertising creative director Luke Sullivan tells the story of a TV commercial created by the Martin Agency, one of the most creative ad agencies in the business. The client made an insecticide called Ammo. But because Ammo was cheaper than the competition, people thought it wasn't as effective at killing worms. The creative team had the brilliantly simple idea of showing two sledgehammers lying side by side on a seamless white background. One of the hammers was made of iron. The other looked like it had been forged from solid gold. Sitting next to the two hammers were two tiny worms. The voice-over says, "You have your expensive insecticide." A hand comes in. Picks up the gold hammer. Flattens one of the worms. Then he says, "And your cheap insecticide." Hand comes in. Grabs the iron hammer. Smashes the other worm. Voice-over: "So. Which worm is more dead?"

> It's easy to think that big ideas and big budgets are synonymous. But it's far from the truth.

This was not an expensive commercial to produce. There were no special effects. No soft drink machines being dragged up on a tractor beam into an alien starship. No rock stars. No World Series MVPs. The voice-over wasn't a movie star. John Williams didn't write the music. Come to think of it, there wasn't any music. There were none of the things that can and often do drive up the cost of producing a TV commercial. But there *was* an idea. The company was constrained by the box of its low budget and yet came up with a great spot.

Most people know about the Cannes Film Festival, where every year the international movie industry honors its own. Less well known, unless you're in the business, is the annual Cannes International Advertising Festival. Ad people love awards and awards shows, but a Cannes Lion is one of the most sought-after prizes of them all. In 2005 the number of entries in the festival was down from recent years; this was thought to be the result of widespread budget cuts in agencies around the world. No argument there. But then Adforum.com, a popular advertising website, asked this question, "Cannes has seen a decrease of its entries this year, due to adverse economic conditions. Do you think that these conditions have changed the level/nature of creativity of advertising? In what way?" I was floored by this. What was Adforum suggesting, that unless you had a seriously big budget to work with, you might as well forget about winning a Lion? Ridiculous. Money is not now, has never been, and will never be a substitute for a great idea. Can it make a great idea even greater? No. It can make it more visible. It can make it louder. But greater? Not at all. And fortunately, I wasn't the only one who thought so. Here's what some of the people in the forum had to say:

> *"When you have less money to work with, you tend to have to dig a little deeper to get to the essence of your message. It can be a catalyst for the unconventional."*

> *"When you look at a wall of twenty different concepts and have to pick your best three—chances are they are the simplest and the cheapest to produce of the lot."*

"There were some creative solutions that transcended budget limitations, and stood up next to expensive productions, simply because a great idea was there."

"Maybe the brain is forced to imagine more interesting things with less budget. Picasso used to say, 'If you have green, paint with green. If you have red, paint with red. But use what you have on hand.' To create a masterpiece, all you really need is a great mind. And as Michelangelo expressed it, 'Art lives on constraint and dies of freedom.'"

Was Adforum alone in assuming that somehow cuts in advertising budgets inevitably lead to cuts in creativity? No it was not. A lot of companies believe that the fewer resources available to them, the less they can dedicate to innovation. Maybe you or your company believe this. That is a problem, because if you really believe that big, enormous, monstrously wonderful ideas will never happen for you because you don't have the financial resources of an Apple or a Motorola or an eBay or the neighbors down the street, then you are denying yourself tremendous opportunities for growth and satisfaction. All it takes is an acceptance that ideas are their own power source. They feed on themselves. They happen because someone just sits down and connects some dots that no one thought to connect before. Knowing that money is tight. Knowing that limited resources will make some dots unconnectable. And yet also knowing that, if they just keep looking, they will always find plenty of dots inside that seemingly tiny box.

Houdini in Wonderland

Inarguably, Walt Disney was one of the most creative forces in the history of American business. Even now it's almost unimaginable that one man's imagination could have bred the $60 billion television, publishing, retail, and theme park empire we know today. Every year the Walt Disney Company pours millions into new creative undertakings. But it was a much different story for Disney himself.

Like so many creative people, Walt Disney saw money as a means to an end. Of course, in Disney's case, the end was always the realization of a vision. What that meant was that there never really was an end, since Walt was constantly coming up with new ideas.

There are a couple of great examples of how Walt Disney was able to maintain his creative focus despite a formidable shortage of financing. It was 1921. Walt, determined to make a living as a cartoonist and after managing to raise $15,000, started a tiny company called Laugh-O-Grams. Not long after, the fledgling animation studio got an assignment from Pictorial Films to produce a series of cartoons for $11,000 with a down payment of $100. The future was looking good. But six months later, the bottom dropped out when Walt's client declared bankruptcy. Needless to say, other than the $100, Laugh-O-Grams never saw a dime of income for all its work. Unable to pay their salaries, Walt had no choice but to let his employees go. Because he couldn't pay the rent on his apartment, he was forced to move into the studio. Had the owners of a Greek restaurant in his building not felt sorry for him and extended him credit until he got back on his feet, the young Disney would surely have gone hungry. And yet, under all that financial pressure, Walt's imagination never skipped a beat. With $500 he got from doing a dental hygiene film for a local school, meager though that sum was, he poured every nickel into an animated feature he called *Alice's Wonderland*. The little film was a success. The money started coming in. Walt was on his way. Or so you would think.

In 1927, Disney created a series of cartoons featuring a character Walt had dreamed up called Oswald the Lucky Rabbit. After making twenty-six Oswald cartoons, Walt wanted to keep the series going for another year. But when he went to his distributor to get additional funding, the news wasn't good. Not only was it not willing to invest another penny in Walt, but as Disney quickly discovered, the company had hired away most of Walt's animators, hoping to produce the Oswald cartoons themselves at a lower cost. And because the distributor owned the rights to the character, there wasn't a thing Walt could do about it. Again Disney found himself staring down the barrel of financial ruin. But true to form, he never flinched, instead keeping his creative focus on imagining a new character, one that would be even more popular than Oswald the Rabbit.

At first the reception to Mickey Mouse was lukewarm. While distributors liked the character, the first two cartoons that Mickey appeared in were silent films, and that was a problem because sound was all the rage and it was sweeping through the motion picture industry like wildfire. Yet another obstacle. But again Walt showed his creative resiliency by making a third Mickey Mouse cartoon, this time with fully synchronized sound. On November 18, 1928, *Steamboat Willie*, the first talking cartoon in history, opened to rave reviews at the Colony Theater in New York. For Walt Disney there was no looking back after that.

Money Doesn't Make You More Creative

Few people would disagree that Walt Disney was an extraordinarily creative person, but as you can see, Disney also demonstrated an incredible level of creative flexibility, especially when the financial walls were closing in on him. Truly creative people, the ones who consistently generate real ideas that solve real problems in elegant and electrifyingly innovative ways, all have this ability to zone out dollar signs. It's as if they are wearing some sort of creative blinders that force them to see the idea and nothing but the idea. Their budget can be the size of a neutron. Somehow they just don't see it. It's not that they aren't aware of it. They are. They just don't let it contaminate their thinking.

> It's as if they are wearing some sort of creative blinders that force them to see the idea and nothing but the idea.

It's like James Earl Jones says in *Field of Dreams*, "Build it and they will come." He was talking about a baseball field, of course. But it's good advice for thinking creatively, too. Don't get distracted by something you may or may not be able to control. Just put on the blinders and turn your mind like a laser beam on the problem you're trying to solve. Build a big idea. The money will come.

But once it does, what then? What if, despite the constraints on you financially, you're fortunate enough to come up with your own Steamboat Willie. And what if, as a result of that idea, whatever it might be, you suddenly find yourself with just the opposite problem? I know it's difficult to understand how too much money can be just as big a creative stumbling block as too little. But it can be, and it is.

I've already mentioned Fallon McElligott Rice, the upstart ad agency in Minneapolis that turned the advertising industry on its head in 1981. Had you asked someone working at one of the megalithic agencies on Madison Avenue what the chances were of Fallon McElligott Rice making it on the national stage, I'm willing to bet they would have said slim to zero. Oh, they'd probably do all right in Minnesota. Maybe, if they were really lucky, the fledgling agency might even do well in the wider Midwest region. But in the end it was as plain as the nose on your face. Like every other small agency in America, Fallon McElligott Rice didn't have a prayer of becoming anything more than just another podunk shop, forever relegated to working with pesticide companies, car dealerships, and the local savings and loan. And really, without big clients with big budgets—well, how far could you go?

At first it seemed like the conventional Madison Avenue wisdom would turn out to be right. The young Minneapolis shop did in fact work with small clients with small budgets. But like Walt Disney, Fallon McElligott Rice chose to focus on doing great creative work despite its lack of money. In fact, the agency embraced its small budgets and found ways to think more creatively and come up with more innovative ideas than its competitors. Embracing its boxes became the agency's greatest strength.

And it worked. FMR quickly made a name for itself, not just in the Midwest but all over the country. Before long, bigger clients came knocking on its door. National clients with deep pockets. And it didn't stop there. Other creatively driven, regional agencies began popping up in off-the-beaten-path cities like Portland, Oregon, and Richmond, Virginia, and Providence, Rhode Island. The big shops in New York didn't get it. How were a bunch of runts from the hinterlands eating into their territory? How were those insignificant little low-budget TV commercials wiping the floor with Madison Avenue's big-budget extravaganzas? It was insane. It was impossible. It was not in the natural order of things. But it worked because all of these companies were able to embrace the boxes of their own financial limitations.

You would think that the success of Fallon McElligott Rice and other small, creatively driven agencies would have lit a fire under Madison Avenue. It did not. At least, not right away. Ideas continued to take a backseat—a very distant backseat—to glitzy special effects, exotic locations, popular songs, and celebrity actors and athletes, many of whom never even appeared on camera.

Nowhere was this kind of blind infatuation with technique over concept more apparent to me than in the following story. The client was a car company. It was launching a new luxury brand. This was right around the time when Acura, Lexus, and Infinity were making their moves in the United States, and so, of course, the client was concerned that, unless the advertising made some serious noise, it could easily get lost in the shuffle. So what did the agency do? It did not come up with a big idea, I can tell you that. But it did come up with the idea of hiring a big-name Hollywood movie star to do the voice-over. Not that there's anything wrong with that. On the contrary, a celebrity can bring an added dimension to a big creative idea. The mistake comes when you try to make a celebrity *the* dimension. So is it a mistake to spend $2 million for a movie star's voice? Not necessarily. Is it a mistake if that movie star's voice is so nondistinct that nobody recognizes it and that a struggling actor off the street you could have gotten for far less money would have been just as effective? Yes. That's a mistake. But it's a mistake that even professional creative people can and do make, and it's not hard to see why. But just as the Sixth Street Photography Workshop and Walt Disney have demonstrated how a lack of money doesn't have to be a barrier to innovation, neither should an abundance of it. Don't delude yourself into thinking that creativity cannot exist without money.

> Don't delude yourself into thinking that creativity cannot exist without money.

A Little Less Creative Freedom Can Go a Long Way

Unless you have the discipline of a monk, I am absolutely convinced that big budgets are potentially far more poisonous to coming up with big ideas than are small budgets. So much so that even if you have an inexhaustible source of funding, you need to consider imposing artificial financial restrictions on yourself. Just take the temptation off the table. Just cut it right out of the process. You'll be amazed at how the entire creative process clicks up a notch as a result.

In 2005, the movie industry had one of its worst summers in history. Nothing seemed to break it open like in summers past. There was no *Spider-Man*. There was no *Jaws*. No *Indiana Jones*. There had been hopes that maybe *War of the Worlds*, Steven Spielberg's interpretation of the H. G. Wells classic, might have pulled it off, and though the movie did well, it didn't really resonate with audiences as DreamWorks SKG had obviously hoped. *The Fantastic Four*, the movie version of the Marvel comic, fared no better. Even *Star Wars: Episode III—Revenge of the Sith* seemed to lack the excitement, and the box office, of the original trilogy.

If the movie industry was surprised by this, it shouldn't have been. For a long time now, creativity and story have been conspicuous by their absence from virtually every major studio in Hollywood. And the more money they try to throw at the problem, the worse it seems to get.

In 1995, two filmmakers from Denmark, Lars von Trier and Thomas Vinterberg, came to the conclusion, and rightly so, that filmmaking had become overrun by forces that were completely and utterly contrary to what film is supposed to be about. To von Trier and Vinterberg, movies didn't become successful because of their special effects, epic stunts, special lighting, exotic sets, or surround sound let alone their obscenely paid big-name stars. Movies were only truly successful when they had a fundamentally dramatic story. The two Danes realized that the reason few

people were coming up with genuinely creative stories anymore was that far too much emphasis was being placed on
everything but creativity, and that as long as moviemakers
had such expensive technology at their beck and call, the
situation wasn't going to get any better.

Their solution was the Dogme Manifesto, a kind of Ten
Commandments that filmmakers would agree to abide by
and that, if adhered to, would result in a movie that was
focused on storytelling ability instead of technology.

These were the rules:

1. Shooting must be done on location. Props and sets
    must not be brought in (if a particular prop is
    necessary for the story, a location must be chosen
    where this prop is to be found).
2. The sound must never be produced apart from the
    images or vice versa. Music must not be used unless
    it occurs where the scene is being shot.
3. The camera must be handheld. Any movement or
    immobility attainable in the hand is permitted. The
    film must not take place where the camera is
    standing. Shooting must take place where the film
    takes place.
4. The film must be in color. Special lighting is not
    acceptable. If there is too little light for exposure,
    the scene must be cut or a single lamp must be
    attached to the camera.
5. Optical work and filters are forbidden.
6. The film must not contain superficial action—no
    gratuitous murders, weapons, or chase scenes.

7. Temporal and geographical alienation are forbidden. That is to say, the film must take place here and now.
8. Genre movies are not acceptable.
9. The film format must be Academy 35 mm.
10. The director must not be credited.

Here's the interesting thing. Most of the rules in the Dogme Manifesto actually amount to a limitation on budget. No special lighting can be used. No extraneous props can be brought onto the set. No studio-recorded music can be included. All of it was completely alien to the way movies were conventionally made. Because of the enormous budgets the big production companies had at their disposal, they could afford to spend a fortune on special lighting. If they wanted to build a pyramid in the middle of Death Valley, they could do it. If George Lucas wanted to get John Williams to conduct the London Symphony on a soundstage at Skywalker Ranch in Marin County, he could.

What von Trier and Vinterberg did was essentially to say, "Hey, wait a second. Just because we *can* spend all this money, does that mean we *should*? Have we gotten so enamored with explosions and car chases and laser battles that we've lost sight of our ability to tell a great story? Have we let technology become a crutch?" The Dogme Manifesto was an attempt to pull the crutch out from under filmmakers and force them back into a much more creative place. It wouldn't be easy taking what amounted to a cinematic vow of chastity, but von Trier and Vinterberg were convinced that the only way to get back to more creative film-making was by going back to a time when movies relied on ideas, writing, and direction and less on how realistic that mushroom cloud rising over Baltimore looked.

Unsurprisingly, Hollywood didn't pay much attention to the Dogme Manifesto. But the message was out and film-makers began to see that the artificial straitjacket imposed by the manifesto was incredibly liberating. The first film to be shot under the Dogme rules was *The Celebration*, directed, appropriately enough, by one of Dogme's original founders, Thomas Vinterberg. *The Celebration*, the story of the trials and tribulations of a big Danish family, managed to catch the eyes of a number of critics in 1999, making it onto their Best of the Year lists. In addition, the film went on to win numerous awards, including the Jury Prize at Cannes and Best Foreign Film at the Independent Spirit Awards.

It didn't stop there. Again the Dogme Manifesto proved its wisdom, this time with a movie called *Italian for Beginners* by director Lone Scherfig. The movie was a hit with audiences at film festivals, including Berlin, where it won four awards, among them a Silver Bear. And like *The Celebration, Italian for Beginners* was a critical success as well. "Its cast of characters may be a little cute," wrote Susan Gerhard in the *San Francisco Bay Guardian*, "but by the time they get together for a well-earned metaphorical big group hug in the form of an Italian-class field trip, you'll forget your fear of handheld camera."

The *Village Voice* agreed. J. Hoberman said, "The film takes the chill out of the Danish winter with a snuggly blanket of humanism . . . you'd need to be a tougher cookie than me to resist the pastor's helpless, benevolent gaze (and surprise tattoo) or the Italian beauty's inexplicable but radiant devotion to a bumbling Dane a dozen years her senior."

Because they were working in a financial straitjacket, Vinterberg and Scherfig and numerous other Dogme filmmakers were able to focus on human stories and little else. All the films were shot on a shoestring. And creatively, they were the better for it.

A Big Idea Can Make Money; Money Can't Make a Big Idea

By now it should be clear that, like all the other alleged obstacles to creativity, money has little to do with great ideas. That's the wonderful thing about ideas. They don't care if your budget is the size of a walnut. They are what they are. They exist or they don't. You can throw all the money you want at a bad idea, and all you'll have is a really expensive bad idea. As Walt Disney understood so well, you can't stop great ideas from happening. They have a life of their own. Disney came to the brink of personal bankruptcy, but even this never interfered with the creative process, just as small clients with small budgets didn't interfere with Fallon McElligott Rice's ability to create compelling, award-winning advertising and if anything only fueled it.

> You can throw all the money you want at a bad idea, and all you'll have is a really expensive bad idea.

If you are to truly become a Houdini Solution thinker, you have to be able to do the same. Don't throw in the creative towel because your budget isn't as big as you think it needs to be. On the contrary, be thankful that it isn't. Think of the great time you had when you were backpacking across Europe with $10 in your pocket and not much else. Think of the Sixth Street Photography Workshop and the brilliant work that resulted from austerity. Think of your sister's wedding, when she and her husband were married barefoot on the beach and then had an intimate clambake. Think of that gold sledgehammer and the worms in the Ammo TV commercial. Had it not been for his creator's financial problems, Mickey Mouse might never have seen the light of day. So many extraordinarily creative ideas owe so much to meager resources.

So how do you actually do it? How do you put on the blinders and focus more on ideas and less on money, whether you've got too little of it or too much?

1. **Define your space.** Draw a box on a sheet of a paper. Outside the box, write down all the things that you know would be expensive and consequently prohibitive. For instance, if I were getting ready to do a TV campaign for a really small client, my list might include: Must Shoot Locally; No Celebrities; No Big-Name Director; No Original Music. That kind of thing. It's amazing how your brain self-edits ideas once you tell it where it can and cannot go. And that is how creativity is born.

2. **Peel the onion.** Almost everything in life is more complicated than it needs to be. Simplicity doesn't seem to come naturally to too many people. But the chances

are, the simpler the idea, the cheaper that idea is going to be to execute. The key is learning to peel the onion, stripping away the layers of thinking that don't really add anything to an idea. Again, if I were writing a TV spot, if I had something in my script that said, for example, "Open on a 1940s ballroom where a digitally edited-in Benny Goodman is conducting a twenty-piece orchestra," I might change that to something like, "Open on a 1940s barroom where some guy is playing piano." While the 1940s ballroom would be more spectacular visually, it would take weeks of scouting and a pretty heavy travel bill. As for Benny Goodman, his estate would likely want a big fee for using his likeness in a commercial. And needless to say, some no-name piano player nobody's ever heard of is a lot less costly than a twenty-piece orchestra. That's peeling back the onion. Does it ruin the idea? Ninety percent of the time it does not. So don't be afraid to peel.

> The key is learning to peel the onion, stripping away the layers of thinking that don't really add anything to an idea.

Do you really need theater tickets when you might enjoy a free concert in the park instead? Do you really need a four-course meal when a good slice of pizza will do? Accept the limitations money puts on your life, accept your box, and you'll be amazed by what you discover.

3. **Think fast.** If simplicity is the key to thinking creatively on a budget, the key to thinking simply is to race the clock. It seems counterintuitive, doesn't it? There you

are, faced with a limited budget, and now you're going to further burden yourself by consciously limiting your time. But you're really not burdening yourself at all. You're freeing yourself. Think about it. The more time you have to think, the greater the odds you're going to unknowingly expand your thinking, letting it drift off into places it has no business going when money and time are tight. Set a time limit for the project, and that's a lot harder to do. What will happen is that your mind will intuitively get to the simple, and inexpensive, solution.

4. **Choose emotional intelligence over intellectual intelligence.** Bright, highly educated people are invaluable to any organization. But not necessarily when you're trying to come up with a creative idea within a tiny budget. It's not that they can't think quickly. It's that they frequently have issues that can bog things down. I agree with Malcolm Gladwell that smart people often are driven to solve problems in ways that benefit themselves more than the project at hand. "Narcissists typically make judgments with greater confidence than other people and, because their judgments are rendered with such conviction, other people tend to believe them and the narcissists become disproportionately more influential in group situations." For my money, emotional intelligence wins the day over intellectual intelligence almost every time. If you want a simple idea that won't cost a fortune to implement, look for people in your company with a high Emotional Quotient. The higher,

the better. People with a gut instinct that's like something out of "The X Files." Look for those people. Put them on your project. Turn them loose. Watch what happens. After all, did you choose your significant other because you drew up a list of pros and cons, saw what kind of college education he or she had, had this list statistically weighted, and then made your decision? No. You went with your gut. You must do the same thing in business.

7

The Lobsterman and the Lexus

Prejudice cannot see the things that are because it is always looking for the things that aren't.

—ANONYMOUS

I'm sure you know that the FBI has people who are trained to spot serial killers based on how closely they comply with certain identifiable factors. It's called behavioral profiling.

Unconsciously or otherwise, we do exactly the same thing ourselves every day when we make connections, or prevent other connections from being made, based on personal bias and past experience.

For example, you pull up at a local marina in New England and you see a lobsterman get into a Lexus and drive away. Without even thinking about it, if you're like most people, you make a judgment, do you not? Lobsterman. Lexus. There's no connection there. Maybe we've never seen a lobsterman driving an expensive luxury car. We have no reference point. It's not in our experiential database. An old pickup truck, yes. A rusted-out Jeep Wrangler, perhaps. But a shiny new Lexus? It doesn't compute. So, of course, it doesn't fit into our comfort zone of what we believe it is that a lobsterman should drive.

Let's imagine one Friday night after work you and some friends stop by a local bar for a couple of beers. The band is about to launch into its first number. It's a typical small band, the kind you find in bars all over the country: guitar player, drummer, bass player. The guy with the guitar steps up to the mike. The presumption is that what you're about to hear is, well, a guitar. Guitar as in Keith Richards or Carlos Santana or James Taylor. Maybe not as good as what you'd expect from Keith, Carlos, or James, but a guitar nonetheless. And then the guy starts strumming and you're shocked to hear—a saxophone. That's right. A saxophone. It's called a synth guitar, and, like a keyboard synthesizer, it can replicate almost any musical instrument you can think of. We can accept this from a synthesizer. And why wouldn't we? Synthesizers are supposed to replicate the sound of different instruments. But a guitar that sounds like a saxophone, this is a total disconnect. Our preconceptions tell us that only things that *look* like saxophones are allowed to *sound* like saxophones.

Is this a normal thing? Of course, it is. We all do it. It's just how most people's brains work. Nobody means anything by it. It just happens. But at the same time, there could be no worse obstacle to building a culture of creativity in a company. It's this stubborn clinging to the connections we *know* instead of the connections we could *make* that prevents so many organizations from taking advantage of their latent creative ability.

If I were to ask you what business you are in, what would you say? If you ran United Airlines, would you say you're in the airline business? What if you woke up tomorrow morning and you were Richard Branson? Now what do you think your answer might be? Are you still in the airline business? The passenger train business? The music business? Or are you in the delivering-extraordinary-human-experiences business? That might include an airline. But it might also be a luxurious high-speed rail system. It might be a recording label. Or a cellular phone service. It might even be the first commercial spaceflights to the moon. People like Richard Branson see the lobsterman in the Lexus and think, "Yes, I can see how those two things could connect together." This is how the mind of an innovative thinker works.

> It's this stubborn clinging to the connections we *know* instead of the connections we could *make* that prevents so many organizations from taking advantage of their latent creative ability.

Darwin's Theory of Innovation

Once upon a time, there was a company called Dietzgen. If you're old enough, maybe you remember it. Dietzgen made slide rules, which were, for a long time, the premier brand in the slide rule business. When Apollo 11 landed on the moon, I'm willing to bet that more than a few of those NASA engineers in Houston and Cape Canaveral had Dietzgen slide rules sticking out of their back pockets.

But there would come a defining moment for Dietzgen when the company would be asked the same question that I just asked you. *What business are you in?* Unfortunately, Dietzgen didn't have a Richard Branson at the helm. Because if it had, he might have said, "Obviously, we're in the calculator business," rather than, "Obviously, we're in the slide rule business," which turned out to be exactly the wrong answer. Why? Because when electronic calculators began to make inroads, Dietzgen didn't rise to the challenge. The company didn't reconceptualize its box. It didn't see how what it was doing was great and refused to accept the confines of the time and grow. It didn't adapt. Maybe if it had, maybe if it had known what business it was really in, Dietzgen might have come out with its own line of electronic calculators. Instead, Dietzgen remained a slide rule company. Other than as collector's items on eBay, how many slide rules do you think were sold last year? Dietzgen didn't recognize its own strengths, adapt according to its own limitations inside the box, and go from there.

There have been other Dietzgens.

In the late nineteenth century, Western Union was at the top of its game. There was practically no place in the country that Western Union didn't have wired. The telegraph was king. And then one day in 1877, Gardiner Greene Hubbard showed up in the office of Western Union CEO William Orton. Hubbard had a proposal for Orton. Only a year earlier, Hubbard's future son-in-law had succeeded in transmitting an intelligible human voice over a wire. Hubbard felt that the new invention—a telephone was what he called it—might be of interest to Orton. Hubbard told Orton that if Western Union wanted to buy the new technology, he had been authorized by the inventor to sell it for $100,000. Orton wasn't impressed. "What use could this company make of an electrical toy?" The thing was unwieldy, Orton told Hubbard. The cost of wiring tens of millions of homes would be astronomical, and besides, what advantage was there? Who needed to hear someone saying something over a wire when they could just transmit what they needed to say with a telegraph? Bad move on Orton's part. Alexander Graham Bell went on to become an icon of American ingenuity, while Western Union went from the predominant communications company it once was to the money transfer company it is today.

> It's how you connect things—disparate things, things that at first seem odd together—that's at the true core of creativity.

People say there's not much new under the sun. I'm not sure that's true. But it doesn't matter because it's how you connect things—disparate things, things that at first seem odd together—that's at the true core of creativity. It's being able to take something from a Chinese restaurant and put it on the same plate with something from a pizza parlor or a sushi bar or a gelato stand. You realize that all you have is a slice of pizza, some pineapple, and some ham and voilà! The Hawaiian slice is born. You accept what you have and then go with it.

In 1981, a couple of California Polytechnic State University design professors, Don Koberg and Jim Bagnall, wrote a book called *The Universal Traveler: A Soft-Systems Guide to Creativity, Problem-Solving, and the Process of Reaching Goals.* In it Koberg and Bagnall talk about something they call "morphological forced connections." If you're one of those people who still have trouble coming to grips with Felix Unger and Oscar Madison, then I highly recommend you try this.

First write down the problem you're trying to solve. Let's say you work for A. T. Cross and you're trying to come up with a new kind of pen. So maybe you write, "Design new pen." You are limited by the box you've created of designing a new pen.

Next, under your statement of the problem, make a list across the top with all the different attributes of the situation as it currently stands. Because we're talking about pens, what are all the conventional attributes of pens that you can think of? So your list might include things like: cylindrical, ink, roller, ball, cap, retract, metal, plastic, cartridge. Now, underneath each attribute, list as many alternatives for that attribute as you can think of. Under cylindrical, for example, you might have square, triangular, oval, hexagonal. Under metal, you might list wood, rubber, fabric, cork, ceramic.

You've just come up with the walls of your box.

Now go through each column of optional attributes at random, making as many different new combinations as you can, as quickly as you can. Again speed is important. Give yourself a deadline and apply some pressure. The faster you make these connections, the less time you'll have to criticize them.

Finally, when you've connected as many attributes as you can—I'm no math genius, but I can tell you there are millions—now you can be critical. A pen made of concrete that has no cap and a wheel instead of a roller ball might be a terrible idea. But a pen made of marble with an oval barrel with a roller ball that's attached to a miniature spring suspension system might be a great idea. The point is that there are probably hundreds of new pen designs that you can uncover in this way simply by forcing connections that you ordinarily might not make.

Seeing What Nobody Else Sees

I cannot stress highly enough this idea of making connections. Once you begin to see these imaginary links between things, you cannot imagine the ideas that will begin to come bubbling up all around you. You are not thinking outside the box but *inside* it. You are embracing your limitations and thinking about new ways to put them together.

Ever since 1826, the Pilkington family had been in the glass business. By the time the early 1950s rolled around, demand for flat glass was extremely high. Everyone wanted it for its relatively smooth and blemish-free surface. But one day, while washing dishes, Alastair Pilkington noticed how grease floated on top of his dishwater. Most people would have seen nothing more than that. Grease floating in dishwater. But standing there at the sink, Pilkington saw something else. What if the grease were molten glass? And what if the dishwater were some sort of liquid upon which the glass could float? As the glass cooled and became hard, it would be as smooth as the surface of the liquid itself. And he was right. After a bit of experimenting, he found his "dishwater," which turned out to be liquid tin. The float method of manufacturing flat glass was born. And all because Pilkington had seen a connection between grease and glass, between dishwater and tin. He looked at what he had to work with, put them together in a different combination, and became a millionaire.

Clearly, Alastair Pilkington and William Orton are two very different people. Pilkington had no problem connecting a household task with a revolutionary manufacturing process. Orton, on the other hand, had a lot of trouble connecting Bell's "electrical toy" with a revolution in communications that would one day make the telegraph obsolete. The reason is simple. Pilkington was conceptually unbiased. Orton was not. One saw the lobsterman get into the Lexus and accepted the connection, the other saw the same thing and rejected it because of his preconceptions. You cannot build a creative company without people like Alastair Pilkington, people who are able to put aside their preconceptions, if only temporarily, to free their minds to wander and make connections. Remember the A. T. Cross exercise? I didn't say not to be judgmental about the connections you made. I said to hold off on your judgments until later. Preconceptions aren't necessarily a bad thing. They're bad only if you let them interfere with the creative process.

Let's try something. Let's pretend it's 1943. You run a company that makes military fighter planes. For years you've been using rivets to hold your planes together. You trust them. They're light in weight. They're strong. They work. Then one day some guy in a white lab coat walks into your office and says he's got a better idea than rivets. "Great," you think. Of course, what you're imagining he's about to show you is something akin to, well, a rivet. It might be bigger. It might be fatter or thicker. But whatever it is, it's probably a lot like a rivet. Only then he tells you what his big idea is, and it is most definitely nothing

> Preconceptions aren't necessarily a bad thing. They're only bad if you let them interfere with the creative process.

like a rivet. In fact, it is glue. The guy in the white lab coat wants you to glue an airplane together. What's going through your mind in that moment? Either you are thinking, "Wow, what an ingenious idea! Why didn't we think of this before? Think of all the weight we can save. Which means our planes will be faster and more maneuverable." Or perhaps you are thinking, "Wow, what a stupid idea. Who in his right mind would glue a fighter plane together? Glue is for paper dolls. Glue is for putting snapshots in photo albums. Unless you want the wings to fall off, glue is not for combat fighter planes." My guess is that you would have thought the latter. And really, who could blame you? After all, everything in our consciousness tells us that glue, while fine for sticking snowflakes on construction paper in kindergarten and mending broken flowerpots, is probably not strong enough to bond steel. But, of course, as we now know, aeronautic adhesives are not only stronger than rivets, the bond they create is actually stronger than the steel itself.

When you think inside the box, what you're essentially doing is forcing yourself to play the hand you've been dealt. You don't have a lot to work with. But the Houdini Solution doesn't really care about that. What matters is an ability to derail your intuitive prejudice, to look at something that's always been there and see something entirely different.

Defusing a Nuclear Bomb When All You Have Is Chewing Gum

If there is a poster boy for the Houdini Solution, it has to be MacGyver, the character played by Richard Dean Andersen in one of the most popular TV shows of the 1980s. Maybe you remember it. Every week MacGyver would find himself trapped in one seemingly impossible situation after another. But then, somehow, he'd find a brilliantly creative solution to the problem using the simplest things you can imagine.

Like the episode when MacGyver finds himself locked inside a freezer. Using a meat hook, he unscrews the back of the door handle. Then, using some cardboard for a funnel and a piece of metal track he finds, he melts some ice using the heat from a light bulb, runs the water down the track and into the door lock. The water refreezes, expands, and bingo, the door opens. That is the Houdini Solution in action.

Let's try another episode, only this time let's pretend you're MacGyver. I'm going to lay the problem out for you, then I want you to put yourself in MacGyver's shoes and solve it.

In an underground laboratory in New Mexico, a series of explosions traps the workers on the lower levels. They want you to help free any survivors. When you get to the lab, you find out that the blasts have caused a leak in a tank of sulfuric acid, and the acid is going to reach the Rio Grande if it isn't stopped. You have thirty minutes to find the leak and stop it before a bomb designed to seal off the laboratory in the event of an environmental disaster goes off, burying both you and any survivors alive. There's another complication. The lab has a complex security system, so getting to the survivors won't be easy. You decide to go down the elevator shaft. You make it down the shaft to another level of the laboratory. The blasts have torn the place apart. There's debris everywhere. The door to a power switch has been blown off its hinges. A candy vending machine lies on its side. A case containing an emergency fire hose has been shattered. The floor is covered with shards of glass. Even the fluorescent overhead lights have been blown to bits. You go around a corner only to discover the hallway is blocked by rubble. There's a steel girder lying across the top. You can hear tapping from the other side. Survivors!

- **Challenge 1: How do you clear away the rubble so you can get to the survivors?** You make it through. You and one of the survivors find the source of the acid leak.

- **Challenge 2: How do you patch the leak?** You go back to help the other survivors get back to the surface before the device can be detonated. Suddenly, one of the scientists pulls a gun on you. You discover that he's the one who rigged the explosions to destroy the lab so that his discovery couldn't be turned into a weapon. You manage to get the gun away from him and knock him unconscious. But with only thirty seconds left, there's no time to get back to the surface before the whole place goes up in a fireball.

- **Challenge 3: How do you get word to the surface to call off the detonation?**

Well, how did you do?

If you said you would have used the emergency fire hose to move the steel girder, congratulations. That's exactly what MacGyver did. How about the acid leak? If you thought like MacGyver, you would have remembered the overturned candy vending machine, snatched a candy bar, softened the chocolate by clenching it in your hand, and stuffed it in the hole, easily sealing off the leak. Finally, did you find a way to communicate with the surface so they could stop the count-down? Remember, you only had thirty seconds remaining before the bomb was to go off. Seems impossible, doesn't it?

You don't have a walkie-talkie. You don't have a cell phone. Of course, that assumes you need to communicate with your voice. Fortunately, MacGyver assumed no such thing. What about Morse code? That would have worked. But how would you have gotten your message through? If you were MacGyver, you would have remembered the power box. You would have known that by switching the power on and off, every light in the building would go on and off as well. Where most people would have seen a power switch, Mac-Gyver, and hopefully you, saw a Morse code transmitter.

MacGyver, of course, was a TV character. In the real world, very few of us have the ability to see the world without any preconceptions at all.

On May 1, 1981, a jury of eight internationally recognized artists and designers, each of them handpicked by the recently organized Vietnam Veterans Memorial Fund, gathered in an aircraft hangar at Andrews Air Force Base outside Washington, D.C., to decide on the winner of a design competition for the new war memorial. They had been told that the winning design would need to meet four objectives: (1) it would have to be reflective and contemplative in character, (2) it must harmonize with its surroundings, (3) it had to contain the names of those who died in the conflict or who were still missing, and (4) it must not make any political statement about the war.

Over several days the eight gradually worked their way through more than 1,400 entries, whittling them down to 232 and finally to 39. On this final day of the judging, they eventually settled on Entry Number 1,026, stating that the design clearly met the spirit and formal requirements of the program, that its open nature would encourage access on all occasions, at all hours, without barriers and yet would free visitors from the noise and traffic of Washington, D.C. And that, you would think, would have been that.

But it wasn't.

When twenty-one-year-old architectural student Maya Lin submitted her design to the competition, it never occurred to her that the V-shaped wall of polished black stone inscribed with the names of the roughly fifty-eight thousand men and women who were killed in the war or declared missing in action would set off a firestorm of controversy. Almost from the moment the winner was announced and the design unveiled to the public, hundreds of disappointed, some of them furious, veterans began lashing out at Maya Lin's radically stark memorial. Many felt it was an insult to the memory of those who had died. Where was the white marble? Where were the bronze statues of fallen soldiers? Why was it placed below ground, a clear reference to death and loss? And why a wall of all things? Vietnam had been one of the worst chapters in our history. Not since the Civil War had the country been so polarized. Did we really want to be reminded of that wall that had divided us for so long? This wasn't a monument, they argued. Instead of looking like a war memorial, it looked more like something that belonged in an art museum.

Maya Lin didn't see it that way. She gave thought to the limitations on her, embraced her box, and came up with genius. To her the polished black granite wall, its eastern wing pointed toward the Washington Monument and its western wing pointed toward the Lincoln Memorial, represented a bridge between the pain of the past and the hope of the future. She saw it as a park within a park. A place for quiet reflection. An opportunity for visitors to look into its polished surface and see the names of the dead but also to see ourselves. To understand their place in history but also our own. This would not have been possible with a more traditional design approach or had she been given free rein. There would have been nothing special about it. There would have been nothing that said, "Yes, all war is terrible, but this was Vietnam." This was something different, made possible only by the four limitations placed upon her.

Nearly three thousand miles away stands another powerful testament to what is creatively possible when we're willing to short-circuit our preconceptions. The Oklahoma City National Memorial, like Lin's wall, is not what you might expect a monument to the memory of the dead to be. On the contrary, its Field of Empty Chairs is emotionally powerful in a way that no slab of granite or marble could have been. The field consists of 168 simple chairs, one for every man, woman, and child killed when the Alfred P. Murrah Federal Building was destroyed by a terrorist bomb. The smaller chairs symbolize the nineteen children who died in the attack. Each chair sits atop a glass base etched with the name of the victim. Again the architects looked at the restraints they were given by the topography that was selected and worked within those constraints, those boxes, to develop one of the most powerful memorials of all time.

Once you get beyond your preconceptions, you open the door to a torrent of creative possibilities. Once you realize that almost everything in the universe is capable of fulfilling more than one purpose, there is virtually no end to what is creatively possible, even within a very restrictive conceptual space.

If the Houdini Solution is going to work for you, you need to begin to see the world this way. The more limited the pallet of possibilities you're working with, the more important it is that each of those possibilities be able to serve more than one purpose.

Get into the Beginner's Mind

Zen Buddhism talks a lot about getting into the beginner's mind, that state of blissful ignorance when you have no experience, no baggage, and a hundred million ways to solve a problem. This is something you'd think would be a major challenge for a sixty-two-year-old man. Unless he's Burt Rutan.

Rutan has been designing and building airplanes ever since he was a kid growing up in Dinuba, California. A graduate of aeronautical engineering at California Polytechnic State University in 1965, Rutan was a flight test project engineer for the Air Force. Later he ran the flight test center for Bede Aircraft in Newton, Kansas. It wasn't long before he opened Rutan Aircraft Factory in the Mojave Desert and later Scaled Composites, arguably the world's preeminent aircraft design and prototyping company.

In 1986, Voyager circumvented the planet in nine days, flying nonstop to establish a new world record. In June of 2004, Rutan's SpaceShipOne became the first private craft to reach space, winning the Ansari X Prize a few months later. So unique is the design of SpaceShipOne that Richard Branson's Virgin Galactic plans to take passengers into space using ships based on the designs of SpaceShipOne. SpaceShipTwo will allow passengers to glimpse the planet from seventy to eighty miles in suborbit. Most recently, Rutan's GlobalFlyer successfully completed the first solo nonstop, nonrefueled flight around the world.

I will say it again. Burt Rutan is sixty-two years old. He's been designing and building airplanes for most of his life. And yet, if you were one of the billions of people who watched on TV as pilot Steve Fossett brought the radical plane in for her final approach into Salina, Kansas, you would likely agree Rutan's designs are more innovative and awe-inspiring than ever. You would think that after all this time, Rutan would be riddled with preconceptions. And maybe he is. The difference is that he's found a way to corral those preconceptions and stay in the beginner's mind.

The great thing about the Houdini Solution is that even if the number of creative building blocks you have to work with is very small, they can still produce wildly creative ideas, especially if, like MacGyver, you can learn to see something in those building blocks that you didn't see before. A candy bar is suddenly a sealant. A power switch is a Morse code transmitter. Dietzgen couldn't see that. Neither could Western Union. You can. Get past your preconceptions. When you can see a Lexus and not automatically expect the driver to be wearing loafers, chinos, and a Hugo Boss blazer, that's when you'll know you're an inside-the box thinker. A Houdini Solution thinker.

8

Thinking Inside the Toy Box

When I was young I painted like Rafael. It has taken me a lifetime to learn how to paint like a child.

—PABLO PICASSO

When our kids were small, we would take them out to a favorite local restaurant and, of course, the waitress would invariably bring out a box of crayons and a special placemat decorated with comic book characters. If you've been through this, then you know that I use the term "box of crayons" loosely. Crayola sells a package containing 120 crayons. This was not that. This was one of those minuscule assortments so common in restaurants and doctors' offices. At best there would be five, maybe six, crayons, half of which were usually broken or missing.

This might have been a problem if my kids had been grown-ups. You'd likely hear things like "What am I supposed to do with this?" or "This is a joke, right? Five crayons? You cannot be serious." But children do not do this. It just doesn't matter to them. No yellow? No problem. Who says the sun has to be yellow? It can be blue. No pink? Fine. The clown's skin can be purple. A fire truck ends up green. What do you mean, a king's cloak is usually purple? Haven't you ever seen one that's orange? Our kids accepted the limitations of what they were given and created true art.

And it didn't stop there. Once the food came it would always amaze me how quickly a lump of mashed potatoes could turn into the Great Pyramid at Giza, or a stack of pancakes could become a fleet of attacking UFOs hell-bent on the wholesale destruction of the universe as we know it, or a banana could morph into a nuclear submarine. It didn't matter that noodles didn't look anything at all like the tentacles of a giant squid or that broccoli bore only a passing resemblance to Sherwood Forest. They didn't have huge budgets. They didn't have unlimited time. They had less than an hour to play with their food, and they made something with it.

Can You See the Roller Coaster in the Coffee Stirrers?

When we're very young, we're all naturally gifted Houdini thinkers. Our imaginations are in permanent overdrive. If we have limitations on us, we don't see them. And even if we do, it doesn't matter. If someone puts us in a room with nothing but a few pots and pans, a can of Lincoln Logs, and a yo-yo and tells us to build a theme park ride, it won't occur to us that this is patently impossible. That we don't have any little electric motors. That we don't have any little cars with little plastic safety bars. That there aren't any little plastic people. We'll just sit down with the pots and the pans and the Lincoln Logs and

> When we're very young, we're all naturally gifted Houdini thinkers.

the yo-yo, and we'll start building the most incredible theme park the world has ever known. Like Houdini inside his box, we do the most with what we have—and we excel.

But as we get older, something happens. We learn that there's a right way and a wrong way of doing things. Like the math teacher who can't get past the fact that a student found a different way of solving a problem and so the answer, even though it's correct, is somehow flawed because it wasn't arrived at by going down the accepted mathematical path. Year after year the creativity we knew as children is drummed out of us. We stop playing with our food. We look at a sandbox and we see just a sandbox. Not the Sahara Desert. Not the beaches of Normandy. All we see is a sandbox. We work more and play less. And when we do play, it's not the same. Golf isn't play. Neither is tennis or sailing or table tennis. Not the kind of play kids know. Almost nothing we grown-ups do in our leisure time comes close to sparking our imaginations, to taking us away to distant planets or to the bottom of the ocean. We just don't see it anymore. We just don't get it. All of a sudden, instead of six measly crayons being filled with creative potential, they seem woefully inadequate. It happens because as we grow older, we're told there's a "right" way to do almost everything. Not that there might be *different* right ways. So we gradually fall into line. We come to accept that every problem has one solution. There's just no other way. This is how we come to believe that only artists and songwriters and actors and musicians are creative. It happens because when we are very young, we're told to be realistic. We're encouraged to stop imagining things, as if our imaginations were some kind of forbidden room where all sorts of hideous dangers lurked. When you were a kid, did anyone ever tell you to quit being silly? I'll bet someone did. Did anyone ever ask you why you couldn't just be like everyone else? And why do we keep asking all those silly questions? Curiosity, we're told, killed the cat. Of course, what nobody ever told us is that curiosity did no such thing. If anything killed the cat, it was not being curious *enough*. How do you create something without asking questions? What if we did this? What if we tried that? And yet year after year, we get the creative daylights beaten out of us until one day we actually come to believe we don't have a creative bone in our body. We have a creative bone alright. We have a lot of creative bones. Most of us just don't know it.

Most. But not all. Some of us are lucky. Even as adults we seem to have found a way to hang on to that childlike ability to solve problems by playing with them. Sir Isaac Newton once said, "I do not know what I may appear to the world, but to myself I seem to have been only like a boy playing on the sea-shore, and diverting myself in now and then finding a smoother pebble or a prettier shell than ordinary."

Hey, Isn't That a DC-3 Wing in Your Conference Room?

Newton would have had a field day at IDEO. Headquartered in Palo Alto, California, IDEO is one of the leading product design firms in the world. With a client list that includes Hewlett-Packard, Nestlé, Vodaphone, Samsung, NASA, and the BBC, the company is a ferocious engine of innovation, churning out nearly a hundred new products every year, many of which have become an everyday part of life. Levolor blinds. The Palm V. Polaroid's I-Zone camera. The Steelcase Leap chair. Zinio interactive magazine software. The Oral-B toothbrush. They all first saw the light of day at IDEO.

IDEO is as close to a playground for grown-ups as anything you can imagine, starting with what seems like dozens of bicycles hanging from the ceiling. When it became apparent that many of the firm's employees rode bicycles to work, IDEO designed a system of hangers and pulleys that lets its employees raise and lower their bikes to and from the ceiling directly over their cubicles. The company saw what they had and worked with it. Many of the designers at IDEO are in their twenties, bright kids who swear up and down they do their best work while listening to music. Needless to say, not everyone wants to hear Green Day wailing in their ears while they're trying to design a toothpaste tube. IDEO's solution is Spunk Space, a special area for the younger designers where they can play their music as loud as they want, thanks to a vertically mounted wing from an old DC-3 aircraft that acts as a sound-deadening room divider. They knew their employees liked to listen to music, accepted that limitation, and became more creative because of it.

Tom Kelley, the author of *The Art of Innovation* and the general manager at IDEO, is a big believer in play. But he's quick to point out that there's a method to the madness. Like children, IDEO's designers are encouraged to play with their imaginations. But unlike children, millions of dollars are riding on those imaginations. It might look like chaos at IDEO. It might seem like all those employees acting like kids is counterproductive, that nothing of substance can come of it, but in fact, exactly the opposite is true. It's what Kelley calls "productive play," and few companies are as productive as IDEO.

Play is so fundamental to the culture of one marketing firm in Richmond, Virginia, that it took Play as its name. The company Play might well be one of the most innovative corporate creativity consultancies in the world. Like IDEO, Play's offices feel a lot more like a kindergarten than a respected firm that's routinely working with such companies as BMW, Coca-Cola, eBay, Harley-Davidson, and Universal Studios. Vivid colors cover the walls. So do photographs. Lots of them. Go there at lunchtime, and you might well come across a street performer or two. It's not unusual to see employees whizzing up and down the hallways on Razor scooters. And while it might seem like a circus compared with the typical business office, Play exudes a childlike playfulness that is tremendously conducive to creative thinking. It's as if every square inch of the place is begging you to have fun, to try things, to pretend, to make believe, all of it geared toward solving problems in often breathtakingly innovative ways.

I know what you're thinking. IDEO and Play can get away with stuff like this. After all, creativity is their product. But in the real world, it's different. You can't have bicycles hanging from the ceiling in an insurance company. Who in their right mind is going to let people ride up and down the corridors of IBM or Morgan Stanley or Exxon Mobil on a kid's scooter? Not going to happen. And no one is saying it has to. But take a closer look, and you'll find that what IDEO and Play are really doing is providing a culture of fun, a climate that invites playful thinking. Take away the suspended bicycles, the wild colors on the walls, the rotating DC-3 wing, and the scooters, and you would still feel a very real sense that it's OK to play with ideas and to try things and that if you fail there won't be a pink slip waiting on your desk when you get back from lunch. Yes, IDEO is a physical playground for employees. You can see it. You can touch it. But there are virtual playgrounds, too. You don't have to look like you're a creative company. You just have to actually *be* one. You simply have to find a way, despite the limitations, to bring out the inner creative child in both yourself and the people who work for you. And then you have to say, "Go ahead. Play with this. Make believe. Dream. Pretend. Ask questions. Take these crayons. Make something for me. Have fun."

Kids are almost surrealistically imaginative under any circumstances but especially when they're given limitations.

On the first Saturday of every April, timed to coincide with National Science and Technology month, the Rhode Island Robotics Design Project, an extension of the Rhode Island School of the Future, provides a startling testimony to the critical connection between play and creativity. Patterned after an education philosophy practiced by the Learning and Epistemology Group at MIT, Robotics Park is arguably the largest K–12 robotics event in the country. Each year it challenges more than a thousand students to design and build a themed robotic system within a tightly defined range of materials, including tiny electric motors, Legos, and in some cases a laptop computer. To wander around Robotics Park is to truly understand what is possible when you can come at a problem with a sense of playfulness and with a childlike disregard for creative limits.

> Kids are almost surrealistically imaginative under any circumstances but especially when they're given limitations.

Lord of the Rings: The Siege of Helm's Deep is a good example. On a table approximately six feet square, using only Legos, a few tiny electric motors, and a beat-up laptop, a class of fourth graders from a local elementary school were able to re-create a stunningly innovative scene from Tolkien's epic novel. It's all there. Catapults that hurl tiny boulders. Working battering rams. Horses that move. All of it as tightly synchronized as any Disney World show. Looking at it, you'd find it hard to believe that from such a limited list of materials, something this complicated could be constructed by grown-ups let alone a bunch of nine-year-olds. And that is precisely the point. Grown-ups would have looked at that sad little pile of Legos and motors and shaken their heads in frustration. But when you're nine years old, you don't do that. Instead, you pick up the Legos and the motors and you start playing. You start seeing a possibility here, a possibility there. The thought that you don't have enough blue Legos or the motor is too weak never enters your mind. All you know is that someone's come up with the idea of doing a scene from *Lord of the Rings*, this is what you've got to work with, and you're going to have some fun. If your creative options are limited, and they definitely are, you simply don't see it. What you don't know definitely doesn't hurt you if you're nine years old. On the contrary, where grown-ups would look at a Lego block and see a lump of injected molded plastic, a kid looks at that same Lego and sees a cobblestone or a hobbit's dining room table or a cauldron of flaming oil.

The Chain Reaction Machine Challenge

But even the Siege of Helm's Deep entry pales by comparison with the Chain Reaction Machine Challenge. Inspired by a similar event at the MIT Museum in Cambridge, Massachusetts, the contest pits various Rube Goldberg–type devices against each other. Essentially, this is how it works. A string is pulled at the beginning of the first machine, which triggers a series of physical events. Once those events are completed, the machine pulls another string on the next machine in the sequence, which, after completing its series of events, pulls another string, triggering the next machine and so on. The resulting chain reaction continues until all the machines have, in turn, been activated.

A typical reaction might go something like this: The first string releases a windup toy dog that moves slowly along a narrow track. The toy dog bumps into a golf ball that's sitting at the top of a tube. The golf ball rolls down the tube, hitting a small squeaky toy. The toy squeaks. A sound sensor activates a programmable robot vehicle backward. As the vehicle moves, it tugs on the activation string of the next machine. The string pulls up on a lever. The lever flips a ball down a ramp. When it gets to the bottom, the ball hits a tongue depressor. The tongue depressor knocks over a series of dominoes. The last domino to topple falls on a touch sensor. The sensor is attached to a robotic dog, who lifts his leg, which pulls the string for the next machine, and—well, you get the idea.

Just like with the Lord of the Rings exhibit, the Chain Reaction Machine Challenge puts clearly defined limitations on the young designers:

1. Every machine must operate within an area that is thirty-two by thirty-six inches or thirty by seventy-two inches.
2. Every machine must be triggered from left to right.
3. Every machine will be designed according to a specified theme, which must somehow be reflected in the design.
4. Every machine must be accompanied by a handout or published piece for presentation to the judges and distribution to the public.

5. Every machine must maintain activity for at least one minute.
6. Every machine must be transportable.
7. Every machine must have its own power supply.

While the students who participate in the Chain Reaction Machine Challenge are generally several years older, they are no more concerned with the creative boundaries imposed on them than were the fourth graders behind the Lord of the Rings exhibit. Even though they're older, the Chain Reaction kids still don't see a few creative retaining walls as anything more than a minor constriction on their imaginations.

But you're probably thinking, "Yes, but these are children. Play is fine when you don't have anything on the line other than a trophy. But running a business is different. In the real world of making a profit, who has the luxury of thinking like a child? Even if we knew how, how could we justify such a frivolous approach to running a company? It's one thing to be creative when the only thing you've got to worry about is whether you should have the Cap'n Crunch or the Count Chocula for breakfast, but it's entirely different when you've got shareholders breathing down your neck."

Let me introduce you to Kathryn Gregory. In the winter of 1994, Kathryn was ten years old. It had just snowed, and she and her brother were out in the yard building a snow fort. As has been the case for generations, all that snow was bound to find its way up the sleeve of Kathryn's coat, and it did. The problem, of course, was that neither her coat nor her mittens did a very good job of covering up her wrists, and that was where the snow was getting in. So Kathryn came up with an idea—an idea that took into consideration her limitations: something that would cover her wrists the way her mittens covered her hands and her jacket sleeves covered her arms. A wrist mitten, so to speak. The idea was that it would be worn under her sleeves and mittens. It worked. She made more wrist mittens and gave them to her Girl Scout troop. The other girls loved them. From there, one thing led to another. With the help of an attorney, she came up with a brand name, filed for a patent, applied for a trademark, and founded a company. Wristies was in business. In almost no time, Kathryn had purchase and marketing agreements with the Girl Scouts, Federal Express, and McDonald's. In 1997 she personally took Wristies on QVC. The product has been a huge success. Needless to say, Wristies isn't IBM. But it isn't the sandbox either. It's a real business with real challenges, and it came from the playful mind of a ten-year-old. It is that playfulness that, once you reconnect with it, can generate extraordinarily innovative thinking.

For a lot of people, this is a difficult concept to grasp. We grow up believing that work is work and play is play. The two don't have anything in common with each other. As one of my former creative director partners was fond of saying whenever a copywriter or an art director would come in complaining about having to work on a weekend, "That's why they call it work."

But something gets lost when we try to take the fun out of work. I'm a big fan of the Boston Red Sox. I love the game. But I think most baseball fans would agree that baseball, as is true with most professional sports, has lost something. It's just not fun anymore. It's all become so deadly serious. So joyless. It's all dollars and cents now. It's all business all the time. It's getting harder and harder, with the possible exception of Manny Ramirez, to find players who actually look like they're little boys out there and having the time of their lives. Oh, sure, it's great when you've just won the seventh game of the World Series or the Super Bowl

> But something gets lost when we try to take the fun out of work.

and everyone is jumping up and down, pig-piling on top of each other, dumping Gatorade over the coach. But most of the time, it all seems so joyless. I'd like to tell you that it's better in college or high school or certainly Little League. But it isn't. Not when you've got coaches getting into fistfights with umpires over a bad call or parents beating the tar out of each other. This isn't how it used to be. Baseball used to be fun. Not just for Little Leaguers but for major leaguers. Not to pick on the Yankees, but if I could sit you down in front of a TV set and replay, say, a 1950s Yankees game, and then had you watch a current Yankees game, I think you would see a profound shift from the freewheeling joy of the '50s game to a far more deadly serious vibe coming from today's players. In the 1950s there was a romance to baseball. And it came from an attitude that said, "Hey, I might be a pro, but I still play this game like I'm twelve years old." Today baseball players aren't really players at all. How do you "play" at something when it's paying you $10 million a year? I don't think joy and baseball are two words that have ever coexisted in the mind of George

Steinbrenner and probably never will. And it's not just Steinbrenner. There isn't an owner of any team in professional sports who expects to see a bunch of grown men or women running around like they're still kids. Those days are gone.

Once we leave childhood, true playfulness seems more and more elusive. The older we get, the more complicated playfulness becomes until it turns into something that bears little resemblance to the kind of simple play we knew as children.

How else to explain a game like tennis? I live in a town not far from Newport, Rhode Island, home of the Tennis Hall of Fame. My wife plays there with a friend of hers every Friday morning. A few years ago she started playing in a league. The Hall is a pretty serious place. Nothing like the public courts I knew when I was a kid.

One day, while I was waiting for my wife to finish her match, I noticed some little kids hitting balls back and forth on one of the courts. They were pretty young and not very good. But they were definitely having a good time. On the court right across from them was a young couple who looked to be in their late 20s. They were *very* good. That was one difference between them and the little kids. But there was another difference. The couple didn't look like they were having any fun. Later, during a break, I overheard them talking. You know what they were talking about? Stroke production. That's it. Stroke production. Here's the thing. I don't care if those two were the second coming of Jimmy Connors and Martina Navratilova all rolled up into one ruthless winning machine—they were not tennis "players." The kids were. All the couple saw was hitting the ball over the net.

While it's sad in some ways that a simple game like tennis or baseball should get to the point that it loses its sense of joy, they *are* games after all. So if you don't mind turning your back on the pure fun of the game, that's your choice.

But it's different in business. If you're serious about being a more creative company, you can't afford to be George Steinbrenner. You're stuck in the box, but somehow you've got to give your employees permission to go out and play. Again I'm not suggesting you turn into IDEO. You don't have to paint your walls electric green or pipe in Led Zeppelin or hang an authentic replica of a World War II buzz bomb from your lobby ceiling. What I *am* suggesting is that you let joy happen. Let your employees and everyone else in your life be twelve years old. Let them pull ideas apart. Let them fall. Let them get back up again. Let them have so much fun with a project that they live it and breathe it. Let them play baseball without grown-ups around.

All Work and No Play Makes Jack a Lazy Thinker

If you've ever been an entrepreneur, then you know that in the beginning there's a definite sense of fun in the air. Yes, companies are launched to turn a profit. But they're also started because of a need to break off from the mother ship, to fly solo, to see if they can pull off doing their own thing. I can't speak for Bill Gates or Steve Jobs, but I wouldn't be surprised if both men had more fun when they were just starting out than they are having now. That's not to say that they're unhappy with the way things turned out. Who in their right mind would be? But there's a fundamental energy when something is new and untested. There's no baggage yet. No heavy yoke of responsibility. In those early days of a company, before any of that has a chance to take root, there is a kind of electricity that sparks off everyone involved. It's work but it's not work. It's heavy yet it's as light as a feather. It's fun!

Early in my career three friends and colleagues of mine walked away from their jobs at the advertising agency where the four of us had worked together for several years and started a company of their own. From the moment I heard the news, I had no doubt that I wanted to jump ship, too. The agency where we had worked had gotten stale, out of touch, and it had sunken deeply into a massive rut. It wasn't fun anymore. And if you can't have fun in advertising, where can you? Three months later I turned in my resignation and joined Leonard Monahan Saabye. It was the right move. From the beginning LMS was one of the most playful agencies I've ever worked for. *Especially* in the beginning. Those first months were wildly energizing. All we had to focus on was the simple act of creating extraordinary advertising. There wasn't a big payroll. Our offices were nothing fancy, and it didn't matter one bit to us. It didn't matter that some of us had to type on top of overturned packing crates or that we had to share the agency's only two phones or that because we couldn't afford a refrigerator, we once had to keep an ice cream cake in the stairwell because it was the only place in the office that was cold enough. Fortunately, it didn't matter to our clients either. We were, after all, the young creative lions, and that's what they were paying for. It was enormously liberating to realize that everything was simple and primitive and that we had nowhere to go but up. There was nothing in our corporate past to weigh us down because we didn't yet have a corporate past. What I felt about my work and my life during those first months with Leonard Monahan Saabye, I hadn't felt since I was a kid. Several years later I would leave LMS and start my own agency, and again that fledgling year would be just as scintillating for all the same reasons. I imagine it's the same with every entrepreneur. And in some sense, I think it explains why so many eventually leave the companies they founded and start new ones. Entrepreneurs are a lot like kids. Once something isn't fun anymore, why play? The trick is creating that feeling in any company, big or small, new or old. How do you turn the clock back for every employee and give them permission to think like a kid again?

> Once something isn't fun anymore, why play?

As we've already seen, for companies like IDEO or Play, not to mention almost any top creative advertising agency in the country, this is scarcely a problem. It's a lot easier to think creatively when you're surrounded by an atmosphere that all but breeds it. And there's no question that thinking inside the box becomes a lot easier when the box you're actually working in is fun. But what if you run a company that just won't allow that kind of freewheeling, playful atmosphere that makes IDEO and Play such inspirational workplaces?

For one possible answer to that question, come with me to Catalyst Ranch in downtown Chicago. Catalyst is one of a growing number of off-site creativity workspaces where companies can bring their employees to brainstorm ideas in a climate that's far more conducive to playfulness than the average corporate office. Matchbox cars, tiny puppets, and other toys litter every meeting room. The walls are either of exposed brick or painted in bold, provocative colors. There are blue couches and purple lamps. Meeting areas are occupied by inviting orange, green, and yellow chairs informally strewn around casual throw rugs. All the usual business tools are there: whiteboards, pads of paper, pens, pencils, markers. But so too are crayons, hula hoops, and Play-Doh. If Catalyst Ranch seems oddly familiar, you only have to go to any kindergarten class to see why. Everything about the place is designed to get corporate executives to think like children.

It's the same at Thinkubator, also in Chicago. Thinkubator, run by SolutionPeople as part of its creativity consulting business, is widely considered to be the grandfather of the off-site creativity workspace movement. Like Catalyst Ranch, the quirky meeting area located in a sprawling loft in the West Loop goes out of its way to create what is essentially a corporate playground. Besides the high-speed Internet access, electronic whiteboard, and wall-mounted flip charts, there's a professional karaoke system; bean bag chairs; oversized chair sculptures in the shape of lips, feet, and question marks by French artist Louis Durot; and a complete Sony PlayStation 2 video game system. Even the restrooms, with their Albert Einstein and John Travolta themes, are designed to encourage creative thinking.

The Houdini Solution is about pulling an end run on the barriers we all have to our creativity by taking a positive attitude toward them. And I would certainly not argue that most business offices, with their conservatively designed environments, aren't always the most inspiring places to work. With places like Thinkubator and Catalyst Ranch, even the dullest, most drab office need not get in the way of giving your employees a place, if only occasionally, to play, to have fun, and to set free their inherent creative power.

But even if you don't have a Thinkubator or a Catalyst Ranch near you, you can do the next best thing. Why not set up your own creativity sanctuary right inside your company or even your home? Is there a spare room somewhere that you could dedicate to company brainstorming sessions? Could you make it different than any other space in the office? Could you paint the walls in bright colors? Could you put some toys out? Some colorful markers?

For example, there's a company in Los Angeles called BRC Imagination Arts that designs what they call brand experiences. They worked on Test Track at Epcot and most recently created the new and highly interactive Abraham Lincoln Presidential Library and Museum in Illinois. Inside BRC's main conference room is a table covered in white butcher paper, where people can write down ideas, make sketches—put down anything at all that comes out of the concepting and design process. As the paper gets filled up, it simply gets rolled up and replaced with fresh paper. The idea is to create a space that is totally contrary in look and feel to where people are used to working.

This space, whether in your business or home, doesn't have to be goofy. There's no rule that says the sanctuary has to be silly looking. Some of the hippest advertising agencies in the world have offices that emote a sense of creative energy without crossing the line into goofiness. The idea is to surround people with an atmosphere that allows them to be creative without trying to impose it on them.

We were all children once. We had imaginations and we had ideas and we didn't care how many crayons were in our crayon box or that our spaceship was really a salad bowl or that the ratty stuffed animal our dad won at the carnival didn't look anything like a unicorn.

We didn't care then.

And we shouldn't care now.

Houdini Didn't Invent Magic; He Reinvented It

Many ideas grow better when transplanted into another mind than in the one where they sprang up.

—OLIVER WENDELL HOLMES

It never fails to amaze me when I hear people say they just aren't capable of coming up with big ideas. What they don't understand, of course, is that very few people are. Even professional creative people like myself. We're all in a box. In my entire career, I can honestly say that I have come up with two, maybe three, genuinely huge ideas. The rest were anywhere from, shall we say, pleasingly plump all the way down to teetering on the edge of pretty darn thin. The same is true for some of the most highly lauded and successful people in advertising.

The fact is, creativity isn't always about the big idea. In fact, it seldom is. Whoever said there's nothing new under the sun knew what he was talking about. I guarantee you that, with very few exceptions, even the best ideas have been done before. And it's that way in almost every field of human endeavor: music, art, literature, relationships, science, and yes, even business.

> The fact is, creativity isn't always about the big idea. In fact, it seldom is.

I remember the first time I heard the Rolling Stones do "Route 66." It was such a cool song. So gritty and rebellious. I had never heard anything like it before. But of course, as I later discovered, the Rolling Stones weren't the first to perform "Route 66." Nat King Cole was. What I didn't know then was that bands like the Rolling Stones, the Yardbirds, John Mayall's Bluesbreakers, Cream, and Canned Heat had simply embraced their limitations and then reinvented and repackaged the blues for a young white audience who, until then, wouldn't have known Muddy Waters if they had tripped over him. And of course, the blues as an art form traces much of its own existence back to Africa and Europe.

The Transplanted Idea

Sometimes an idea can seem so spectacular, so incredibly ingenious, we're certain it could never have been done before. I felt that way when I first saw a certain TV commercial for Honda. Remember those Rube Goldberg–type machines in the Chain Reaction Machine Challenge that I discussed in the last chapter? The Honda commercial wasn't much different. In the spot a series of automobile parts—gears, windshield wipers, tires, and dozens of others—gently nudge each other, creating a chain reaction until finally it ends at a Honda as the voice-over says, "Wouldn't it be wonderful if everything just worked." In 2004 that commercial, named "Cog," took the advertising business by storm. It took top honors at nearly every major creative awards show in the world, including the Palm d'Or at the Cannes International Advertising Festival. Agency people from New York to Singapore couldn't stop raving about this brilliant piece of work. And it *was* brilliant. I had never seen anything like it, certainly not for a car. It was charming. It was memorable. It was a breakthrough idea. Or was it?

In 1987, Peter Fischli and David Weiss created a piece of kinetic art that involved what they called a chain of events. Like the Honda commercial, it involved a series of objects set into motion by other objects, including a series of tires that roll up an incline, nudging one another farther and farther up the incline. Unlike the Honda commercial, the entire sequence lasted approximately forty-five minutes and not all the objects in the chain were automobile parts. And also unlike the Wieden+Kennedy creative team who did "Cog," Fischli and Weiss had nowhere near as much money to produce their creation, so, of course, their version was substantially more primitive. But the similarities between the two are striking. If you were to look at them both simultaneously, there is no way you could believe that this was a coincidence. And because the Honda spot was produced nearly twenty years after Fischli and Weiss first unveiled "Chain of Events," it's apparent which was the original idea and which was the derivative.

So did Wieden+Kennedy steal Fischli and Weiss's idea? Or is it possible that the real idea for the Honda commercial was, in fact, to borrow what Fischli and Weiss had started and improve upon it? And, of course, isn't that exactly what Fischli and Weiss themselves had done when they borrowed and improved on the whacky imaginings of Rube Goldberg? Each of these people embraced the concept that most ideas *have* been done before and simply focused on making theirs new, fresh, and different.

In Patrick Smith's animated short film *The Drink*, a boy discovers a magic potion. He takes a drink, and immediately a man in a business suit stretches and twists his way out of the boy's mouth. A second character emerges from the businessman's mouth. On this goes as everything from bishops to clowns crawls out of the mouths of their predecessors. *The Drink* turned out to be a pretty successful film and in fact was an official selection in more than fifty international film festivals. If I were to show you that film and then I were to show you a TV spot for Nike's Air Huarache sneaker, in which a shoe keeps peeling itself back to reveal progressively different shoes, I think you would be hard-pressed not to see a connection between the two. Like "Cog" and "Chain of Events," it's possible Nike's idea for the Air Huarache had nothing to do whatsoever with Patrick Smith's award-winning film. Coincidences like this happen all the time in advertising—and in life. But it's also possible that someone on the team saw *The Drink*, saw how the technique might solve a creative problem, and transplanted the idea into the Nike spot. The person might have relied on what he knew and built from there.

Somewhere in a file drawer in the U.S. Patent Office resides patent number 5,579,430. There are five names listed on that patent: Bernhard Grill, Karl-Heinz Brandenburg, Thomas Sporer, Bernd Kurten, and Ernst Eberlein.

In 1987 the Fraunhofer Institut Integrierte Schaltungen research center launched Eureka project EU147. Led by mathematician and electronics specialist Karl-Heinz Brandenburg, the project sought to develop a technology that would enable high-quality, low bit-rate audio coding. Collaborating with Brandenburg and the Fraunhofer Institut was Dieter Seitzer, a professor at the University of Erlangen who had been working on ways to transfer music using conventional telephone lines. After several years the first MP3 music file was created when Fraunhofer's and Seitzer's audio-coding algorithm was integrated into MPEG-1, an early, low-bandwidth video compression standard, thus enabling the audio data stored on a conventional CD to be shrunk down to one-twelfth the size.

But as innovative as MP3 technology was, it meant little without an MP3 player. It didn't take long before Tomislav Uzelac, an engineer with a company called Advanced Multimedia Products, invented just that. Unfortunately, because of its narrowly focused technology, the AMP MP3 playback engine was slow to catch on until two college students, Justin Frankel and Dmitry Boldyrev, successfully integrated Microsoft Windows into the AMP player. But even then the MP3 player was a commercial nonfactor.

That changed when Eiger Labs launched its MPMan in the United States in the spring of 1998, followed not long after by the Rio. While the Rio wasn't the first MP3 player, it was the first to be taken seriously as a potential threat to the CD player. And for a while it seemed like the Rio was on its way to becoming a runaway success. But there were problems with the Rio. It was complicated to use. It didn't store many songs. And in terms of design—well, let's just say the Rio wasn't exactly on anyone's short list for induction into the Museum of Modern Art.

What happened next is best summed up by the Oliver Wendell Holmes quotation at the beginning of this chapter. "Many ideas grow better when transplanted into another mind than in the one where they sprang up." Was the Rio a good idea? Absolutely. But it was a much better idea when it was transplanted into the mind of Steve Jobs. What had been a good idea suddenly was transformed into a great idea with the development of the iPod. Creatively, the iPod is no different than the Honda commercial. It took a good idea and made it better. It took a powerful concept and evolved it into an unbeatable one. Regardless of what you think of Apple, most people would agree that this is a hugely innovative company. But its brilliance lies more in its ability to improve on existing technology than in coming up with ideas that are unlike anything that's ever been done before.

Does that tarnish your opinion of Apple as an innovative company? It shouldn't. What was the PC before Apple designed "a computer for the rest of us"? The genius of Apple wasn't that it was the first personal computer. It was that it was the first personal computer that mere mortals such as myself could actually use without holding a Ph.D. from MIT or Stanford.

Halley's Comet: Breakthrough Ideas and Other Rarities

Think about it. How many ideas can you honestly say were groundbreaking? That forever changed the world and the way we live? There just aren't that many. The wheel? Definitely. The automobile? Not really. The car was really little more than an evolution of the horse-drawn wagon. The computer? Yes. The laptop? Not at all. The television was an original idea, but what about the portable DVD player? Nice concept. But in the end it, too, is pretty much a derivative one. The DVD player gave us the ability to watch video on a relatively tiny disc no thicker than a wafer. That was convenient. But the television gave us the ability to bring moving pictures into our living rooms, where once there was only radio. That was monumental.

As creative as some of us like to believe we are, we don't so much give birth to new ideas as we do look back on old ones, accept the box that most things have been done before, dress them up in different clothes, and make them our own.

In his book *The Wisdom of Crowds*, James Surowiecki argues that the collective intelligence of groups of people is often more powerful than that of individuals. For years I didn't believe a word of it. *Collaboration* was a dirty word to me. The idea of two or more people sitting in a room trying to come up with a brilliant advertising campaign or, say, the perfect vacation struck me as a ridiculous waste of time and energy. In my experience groups of people gathering to solve a problem was the kiss of death. There were just too many agendas, too many egos, too many personal motives to get in the way of coming up with a really creative idea. As far as I was concerned, the only way to create something great was in a vacuum. Why would you want to team with others? Who needed someone telling you why your idea might not work when you knew in your gut that it would? For years I felt this way. You and you alone had to do it all. This is what I believed for a long time. And it worked pretty well. But as I now realize, it probably could have worked even better if I had known about Linux.

Linux is the computer server software that, instead of being a closed, proprietary system à la Microsoft Windows, is open to manipulation by outside sources seeking to adapt the software to better suit their individual needs. Today more than 52 percent of companies—including Google, Yahoo!, Amazon.com, and many others—have switched from Windows servers to Linux servers. Not long ago this would have been unthinkable, but the allure of Linux isn't difficult to understand. Who wouldn't appreciate the idea of a server that's custom tailored to your company? And what makes that possible is the collaborative nature of Linux. Any programmer can go into Linux, add a line of code here, lose a line there, change this or that, and the result is that what was there before is very often now better.

Firefox was the first Web browser to adopt the Linux model, in that it was created with the intent that anyone with a knowledge of code would change it, mold it, and shape it into something slightly different. The philosophy that led to both Linux and Firefox is called open source. As business is quickly discovering, the open source concept has advantages that go far beyond computer servers and Web browsers.

How Many Steven Spielbergs Can You Fit into a Sneaker?

Butler Shine & Stern, a relatively small but highly creative ad agency in Sausalito, California, recently launched a website called the Converse Gallery for its client Converse Athletic Shoes. On the site consumers are invited to create, shoot, and submit twenty-four-second videos that they feel capture the values and spirit of Converse. The best of these videos can win their creators $24,000 and a chance to be aired on television. Bear in mind, the people making these little films are amateurs. Many of them have never shot anything more professional than a wedding shower. And yet some of the entries at the Converse Gallery are as creative and as well produced as anything you'll find on Madison Avenue. The filmmakers didn't have much to work with, but they embraced their boxes and often created wonderful films. For a creative powerhouse like Butler Shine & Stern, pulling this off was not an easy thing to do.

"We knew that if we were going to open the floodgates for consumers to have a voice, then we were going to have to actually leave them alone and not impose our own aesthetic on them," John Butler told me. "And that in truth was the hard part. In reality, open source creativity is really just a fancy term for giving consumers a voice and a platform for that voice to be heard."

If you own a bicycle, there's an excellent chance it's a mountain bike. You would think that the mountain bike was created by a company like Trek or Specialized or Cannondale. But nothing could be further from the truth. In fact, the mountain bike wasn't considered a commercially viable product until years after its invention. And here's how that came to be.

In the 1970s a small group of hard-core cyclists in northern California started riding on the trails and fire roads in the hills of Marin County. It wasn't easy. Their conventional road bikes with their skinny tires and spidery frames were no match for the rugged, boulder- and log-strewn trails of the mountains. All the cyclists had ideas of what the ideal bike should be. One thought the tires needed to be fatter. Another thought the frame needed to be tougher. Another felt the brakes needed to be beefier. One by one they pooled their different ideas and eventually created something that had not existed before. They all accepted the limitations, the box of what the bicycle was, and tried to make it better. A big idea that began as a lot of smaller ideas. Today mountain bikes account for the vast majority of total bicycle sales in the United States.

It's easy to understand why most people think of creativity in terms of the big idea. Big ideas are flashy. They're sexy. They get written about. They make it onto the nightly news. And they make the people who came up with them famous. But big ideas come with big expectations.

Prior to its unveiling in early December of 2001 on "Good Morning America," Ginger—or IT, as it came to be known—was supposed to be the single biggest technological achievement in human history. Bigger than the Internet. Bigger than the computer. Bigger than motorized flight. Not since the Manhattan Project had an invention been cloaked in so much secrecy. Rumors of the breakthrough had spread like an Ebola virus in a subway car. Whatever IT was, it was going to change our lives forever. Credit Suisse First Boston fully expected that IT would make more money in its first year than any start-up in history and that its inventor would easily be worth more in five years than Bill Gates.

The inventor was Dean Kamen. And IT turned out to be the Segway HT. Arguably, the Segway, as cool a contraption as it is, is nowhere close to the world-altering invention that it was made out to be. Was the Segway a big idea? I believe so. It certainly had the potential to have a profound impact on personal transportation, especially in cities. But nothing short of teleportation, an interstellar starship, or a time machine could have lived up to the expectations that were placed on the Segway. So as exciting as big ideas can be, unless they can live up to the often absurdly outsized expectations placed on them, they can ultimately prove to be far less significant. Smaller ideas might not end up on "Good Morning America," but they can be far more meaningful for that very reason.

Think about it.

When an idea is as high profile as the Segway or iPod, it's out there for all the world to see. And, of course, to rip off. In their book *Blue Ocean Strategy*, W. Chan Kim and Renée Mauborgne make a compelling case for creating markets where there is no appreciable competition. And that normally means having a big, really unique idea. Just know that while that big, unique idea can give you an enormous advantage out of the box, it's visible, it's being talked about, it's on everyone's radar, and everyone will be gunning for it. That's what makes smaller ideas so wonderful. Because very few people know about them outside the company, you can use them to build a competitive advantage.

Drivers, Start Your Imaginations!

In 1977 Peter Wright, Colin Chapman, and Tony Rudd were looking for a way to make their Lotus Formula 1 race cars do a better job of gripping the road, thereby allowing the driver to corner faster.

As with America's Cup racing boats, there were design rules that limited how far the three designers could go. They had a box in which they had to create. With the exception of upside-down wings that resulted in downforce instead of lift, an innovation that was eventually ruled illegal, it was virtually impossible to come up with a big idea.

And then they thought of Daniel Bernoulli.

Bernoulli was the eighteenth-century Swiss physicist who postulated that a fluid flowing through a constriction would increase its speed while lowering its pressure. Wright, Chapman, and Rudd reasoned that, because air is a fluid, if they could shape the bottom of the race car exactly right, they could create an area of low pressure that would, in effect, literally suck the car down to the ground.

After a number of attempts, a scale model was tested in a wind tunnel. The results were beyond anything the three designers could have imagined. So powerful was the suction, it was as if a giant vacuum cleaner had been installed under the car.

To prevent undesired air movement from spoiling the effect, they came up with yet another idea: simple rubber skirts that kept the air passing under the car free of turbulence that would weaken the suction.

Thus was born the first race car to use ground effects. In 1977 the Lotus-Ford Type 78 won four races and narrowly missed winning the title. One year later an improved version, the Type 79, went on a tear, winning a total of four races, nine pole positions, five fastest laps, the Constructor's title, and first and second place, respectively, for drivers Mario Andretti and Ronnie Peterson. On the surface simple ground effects might not have been as big an idea as wings. But you never would have known it from the way the Lotus-Ford car performed.

The Leveragability of Small Ideas

Small ideas have other advantages, too. Because they tend to be more narrowly focused, small ideas often pay great attention to detail.

The iPod is a pretty big idea. And while multicolored faceplates that allow consumers to personalize their iPods are obviously a much smaller idea than the iPod itself, little things like this can help maintain a product's popularity with consumers as well as its momentum in the market. Big ideas might make you rich and famous, but it's the smaller ideas and details that can keep you there.

> Big ideas might make you rich and famous, but it's the smaller ideas and details that can keep you there.

Sometimes small ideas are highly adaptable. An idea that was meant to improve efficiency on the factory floor, with a few tweaks here or there or maybe none at all, might work just as well somewhere else in the company. It happens in advertising all the time. Someone might have a great concept for a print ad, but many times that same idea will work just as well in television, on the Internet, or as a theatrical promo. Small ideas might lack the emotional intensity of a big idea, but because they sometimes can be leveraged, they can often spread throughout an entire company, magnifying their impact.

Again, big ideas don't happen very often. Otherwise, they wouldn't be big ideas. But small ideas live in a much less rarefied atmosphere. And that means more people are more likely to have them and have a lot more of them. That's important. Like a prospector panning a river, the more grains of sand you sift, the better your chances of finding that one gold nugget. And, of course, there are times when small ideas can be the doorway to a much bigger opportunity.

There's an advertising agency, for example, in New York that knows this all too well. I once worked for a much smaller shop that wrested away a major piece of business from that agency when we talked the client into letting us do a tiny project for a tiny division. The idea we came up with, while it was very different, was nothing earth-shattering. A simple promotion to a network of local dealers—that's all it was. Hardly anything to get excited about. Except that the client didn't see it that way. Before we knew it, our little, local dealer campaign was a big, national dealer campaign. It was very successful and had everything to do with us eventually winning the entire account. By embracing our constraints and working with them, we wound up with something much larger than we had hoped for.

Small ideas, often within the framework of larger ones, can challenge you by revealing gaps in competencies and giving the entire organization a new sense of energy and mission.

I once had a client who told me in a briefing that he hoped we would come back with a campaign that made him feel uncomfortable. By that, he didn't mean nutty TV spots with half-naked women mud wrestling in a bar or a bunch of drunk chimpanzees running amok on a basketball court. What he did mean was, "Show me something that holds a mirror up to us. Something that says, look, this is who you guys say you are, so now you have to actually live up to it." The campaign we eventually presented to him was nothing unusual. Certainly, not what I would call a big idea. But it was big enough to reveal that if the company ran it, they would have to rise to an even higher level of customer service. They did run the campaign. And they did rise to that higher level.

What If You're Not Ready for a Groundbreaking Idea?

Have you ever read Carl Sagan's novel *Contact*? Maybe you saw the movie version starring Jody Foster. In it, scientists working for SETI (Search for Extraterrestrial Intelligence) discover a message from another civilization with instructions for building an interstellar spacecraft. Before long the machine is built and humankind is ready to travel to the stars. But the question posed to the viewer is, "Are we as a civilization capable of rising to something as enormous as traveling to the stars?"

Now imagine your company has a big idea. Not an interstellar spacecraft maybe, but something big enough to potentially change your organization in ways it isn't prepared for. Unless you've had experience with groundbreaking ideas like that, the ultimate effect on your company can be both disruptive and destructive.

Small ideas aren't like that. Because they come along a lot more often, they give people a chance to gain experience in both assimilating and implementing them.

Finally, small ideas are sticky. They tend to attach themselves to each other, one idea to the next, like a ball of string that keeps getting bigger and bigger with every new strand that's added to it. You don't need to think outside the box, but you work with what you have. A colleague recently told me about a furniture company executive in Denver who had received several complaints about delivery people damaging customers' walls and floors. The delivery people insisted they hadn't caused the damage. Then she saw a T-Mobile commercial on TV and got an idea. What if the company replaced the delivery people's cell phones with camera phones? That way they could take pictures of the customer's house immediately after making a delivery. If the customer filed a complaint, she would have a documented photographic record that would exonerate the delivery people if no damage had been done or, conversely, would show the exact extent of the damage. Not a huge idea, but a doable, practical one that fit inside the company's budget and frame of reference.

But like I said, small ideas can be awfully sticky, and the camera phone idea was no different. Pretty soon, delivery crews were using the phones to e-mail pictures of narrow staircases or narrow hallways back to the company, where their supervisor could advise them over the phone what to do. The company's shipping department started using the phone to send photographs of damaged goods back to the manufacturer, greatly reducing the time it took to file a claim or order a replacement. Salespeople even got into the act. If the company had just delivered, say, a new love seat, the delivery crew would be asked to take a picture of the customer's living room. Maybe it would show that the customer needed more lamps or an area rug or possibly a side table. What salesperson wouldn't want to know that?

The lesson here is that ideas come in all shapes and sizes. They are almost never truly original. They almost never come out of thin air. And they almost never are the work of geniuses or visionaries. What small ideas lack in size, they more than make up for in volume. In the long run you are much better off with a steady stream of small innovations than a single bolt of creative lightning. The chances of lightning striking twice in the same place might be rare, but believe me, the chances of *creative* lightning doing the same are downright astronomical. It's the small innovations that build an atmosphere of creativity and imagination that one day can very well lead to the big one.

What? You Thought There Wasn't Going to Be Homework?

My history with mathematics has been a checkered one. I flunked high school calculus only to flunk it again in college. I barely survived geometry, and how I survived trigonometry I will never know. The very thought of balancing a checkbook makes my eyes melt. When I started college I had every intention of becoming an oceanographer. Then I discovered that math was involved. That was the end of that. I didn't know who the next Jacques

Cousteau was going to be, but it wasn't going to be me. The point is, I am just not hardwired for numbers. I'm not alone in this. I know a lot of people in advertising—well, other than in the accounting department—who share my hideous incompetence where numbers are concerned.

Just as I am not a natural left-brain thinker, a lot of people aren't natural right-brain thinkers. But just because you're not naturally gifted at something is no reason you can't be better at it and probably a lot better. Who knows? Maybe if I had worked a bit harder at math in college—instead of hanging out at the student union, playing poker and trying to learn "Eight Miles High" on the guitar—I could have managed at least a C, maybe even the occasional B.

As the budding young engineers of Robotics Park so amply demonstrate, we all have an innate creative sense when we're kids. Some more so, some less. But we all have it. It's a sad testament to our society that, unless we pursue careers that nurture that creativity, we slowly get the fire sucked out of us, little by little, until all that remains is a feeble flicker, barely still breathing deep in our subconscious.

The good news is that creativity is like riding a bicycle. No matter how long you've been away from it, you can get it back. Millions of people have done this. Entire companies have done this. You don't have to be Picasso. You don't have to be Bob Dylan. You just have to be willing to believe that somewhere inside you, there is a creative furnace just waiting to be ignited. You can teach yourself and everyone in your company to become a more creative thinker. Maybe

What? You Thought There Wasn't Going to Be Homework?

167

not *brilliant* creative thinkers. But I can assure you that thousands of successful companies have been built on less than brilliant, mind-blowing ideas.

Now here's the *really* good news. If you can become a more creative thinker, you can become a more creative inside-the-box thinker, too. In fact, because creativity inside the box is more focused than creativity outside the box, building a seriously innovative organization suddenly becomes a very achievable goal with the Houdini Solution.

The Houdini 50 is designed to help get you started.

Out of hundreds of creative thinking techniques developed by hundreds of creativity trainers from around the world, the Houdini 50 represents what I believe to be the cream of the crop in creative training techniques. Some are wide-angle strategies, exercises designed to get you thinking creatively in general. Others are intended to get you thinking specifically within constraints.

Let's get started.

1. The Antonym Lens

Pretty much everything you can think of has a counterpart. A polar opposite. Often, coming at a problem from the diametrically opposite perspective can lead to a creative solution.

That's because opposites aren't really all that opposite. They're just two ways of looking at the same thing. Taoist philosophy says that what appear to be two opposites actually are part of a single unified whole and that only human experience artificially divides the world into false dichotomies.

In junior high school, we all learned what an antonym is, a word that is the opposite of another word. Sweet is the antonym for sour. Pretty is the antonym for ugly. Fast is the antonym for slow.

Now pretend that I've given you a pair of special glasses. What makes them special is that when you look through them, you see the polar opposite of whatever it is that you're looking at. So if you look at a campfire, you'll see a block of ice. If you look at a speeding bullet, you'll see a snail.

Now with your imaginary glasses on, look at your problem. See it in the reverse. What does it look like? Write down what it is not. For example, let's say you're trying to come up with a way to improve your delivery times. Looking through the Antonym Lens, write down all the things you might do to make your delivery times worse.

What if you asked your pilots to go on strike? You could hire inexperienced drivers for your trucks. You could shut down 50 percent of your package-sorting machinery for a week.

Now look at all the things you've written down. Do any of them suggest a thought? For example, if you wrote down "hire inexperienced drivers," is there a way you could better train drivers? Is there a creative incentive plan that would reward drivers for delivering packages more efficiently?

It sounds counterintuitive, I know, but try it. Believe me, reversing your problem like this can uncover areas you might not have otherwise thought about.

What? You Thought There Wasn't Going to Be Homework?

169

2. Creative Snowballing

When you're brainstorming, it's easy to drift off course, to stray out of the box. Not that there's anything wrong with this. You can always go back and edit out ideas that spill beyond the box. But if you're on a tight deadline and you need to generate workable ideas in a hurry, this is a great exercise.

Here's how it works.

Someone has an idea. Write it down. Now instead of launching off in a new direction entirely, try coming up with a second idea that's inspired by the first idea. Then try generating a third idea that flows from the second, and so on. Keep going like this, layering one idea onto another.

Let's say you're trying to design a new video camera. Someone has an idea. What if you could make it easy and fast to send videos to friends and family. Someone else suggests that you could include a free postage-paid mailer. Then someone else wonders if a small wireless transmitter inside the camera could automatically send videos over the Internet.

> Like a snowball rolling down a hill, that first idea gets bigger and bigger, each subsequent idea sticking to the one before it.

Like a snowball rolling down a hill, that first idea gets bigger and bigger, each subsequent idea sticking to the one before it. You'll be amazed how many truly innovative concepts you can come up with. And the best part is that a lot of them, although not all, will be real-world ideas that you can use right away.

3. Angel's Advocate

There's nothing wrong with playing devil's advocate. After all, how can you bulletproof an idea if you don't shoot holes in it?

The problem is that some people don't play devil's advocate so much to point out possible legitimate weaknesses in an idea as they do to kill anything that dares to veer from the status quo. When that happens you've got a serious problem, which, if left unchecked, can foster a climate of negativity that can maim, if not kill, any chance of nurturing an innovative workplace.

> How can you bulletproof an idea if you don't shoot holes in it?

I cannot tell you how many extraordinary ideas have been killed before they ever had a chance to see the light of day simply because someone in the room smothered them with skepticism.

That kind of devil's advocacy, of course, cannot be tolerated. It simply can't. If you suspect someone is consciously or unconsciously sabotaging every idea that's put out on the table, do yourself a favor and take that person out of the process.

What's important to understand though is that even the normal and healthy exercise of probing ideas for soft spots can at times seem defeating. A great counterbalance to this is to have someone play angel's advocate.

Instead of asking what could go wrong with an idea, try asking what could go right. Ask yourself, "If we did something like this, what other problems might it solve? Could it be the catalyst for an even bigger thought?" I can tell you

What? You Thought There Wasn't Going to Be Homework?

171

that it often turns out that way. A little positive reinforcement can have an extraordinary effect.

4. The Incredible Shrinking Problem

Thinking inside the box is one thing. But that doesn't mean you have to make that box any smaller than necessary.

In advertising, before a creative team begins a new project, they get something called a creative brief, a document that defines the scope of the assignment. It usually includes a quick overview of the target audience, the objective of the ad, and the key message.

Under key message, most advertising agencies usually have a line that goes something like this: "What is the one single-minded thought that the campaign has to communicate?" A lot of clients struggle with this. They cannot imagine how their very complex objectives can be boiled down to one simple thought. To them, other companies might be able to do this. But their company is different. Their problem is far too complicated.

This is almost never true. No matter how complex a creative problem might seem to you, someone else can look at that problem and see not 167 colors but one. Most advertising creative people have a natural talent for doing this. And it's a good thing they do, because the best advertising usually tends to spring from the simplest ideas.

You can do this, too.

Write down as best you can what the problem is you're trying to solve. Do this in twelve words or less. In some cases, this might not be all that difficult. But if you're finding it difficult, go back and start editing out everything and anything that doesn't drive the statement forward. Keep shrinking what's left until you get to those twelve words. Your problem will be a lot more sharply defined. And so will your solutions.

5. The Rolling Wall

Boxes aren't necessarily stagnant things. Sometimes those walls that seem so rigid are in fact fairly flexible. The question is, how flexible? You need to know this before you can judge whether an idea fits inside the box or not.

One way to do this is to identify as specifically as you can what the walls of the box actually look like. You do this by first stating your single-minded problem.

Let's say your problem is to design an inexpensive portable wind turbine. Separate the statement into its component parts. In this case, these would be design, inexpensive, portable, wind, and turbine.

Next spend some time with each word and bombard it with questions. For *wind* you might ask if it has to be solely wind-powered. Borrowing from automotive hybrid engine technology, could a small, gasoline-powered engine be added to serve as a backup? When you say "portable," how portable? Portable enough to be transported by a pickup truck? In the trunk of a car? Keep this up for every word on the list. Ask as many questions of each word as you can. Cross-examine everything.

By doing this you create for yourself a high-definition picture of the problem, revealing exactly what it is, what it is not,

What? You Thought There Wasn't Going to Be Homework?

173

and what it can't be. You do this in two ways: (1) you clearly identify the walls of the box and (2) you allow yourself to determine how far, if at all, those walls can be pushed back.

6. We Look, but Do We See?

Assuming you did have the luxury of thinking outside the box—and as you should know by now, this is a luxury few of us will ever know—perspective is not a problem. The bigger your creative landscape, the more ways you can look at a problem.

But inside the box it's different. Suddenly, your perspectives change dramatically. They narrow. They fade. And they certainly become fewer in number.

To prevent this, it can help to bring in a new pair of eyes. A virginal mind that can look at both the problem and the creative boundaries that contain it and that can give you a fresh slant on the situation.

Joey Reiman runs a firm in Atlanta called Brighthouse. Reiman develops marketing strategies for clients like Coca-Cola and Home Depot. A key part of the Brighthouse process is bringing in what Reiman calls luminaries, so called because of the light they shine on creative problems. What's interesting is that none of the luminaries come from a typical marketing background with typical marketing insights. Depending on the project, a group of luminaries could include a neurosurgeon, a housewife, a concert violinist, and a crane operator. The idea works because it forces Brighthouse to gain multiple perspectives and, in so doing, shakes up how they see a given problem.

I once did a campaign in which we photographed different geographical locations from the air. What was interesting was that, no matter how hard you tried, you could not tell exactly what it was you were looking at until you read the ad and discovered that the picture was, say, the Mississippi Delta or the Gulf Stream off southern Florida or something like that.

Thinking creatively inside the box can be just as disorienting. Things might not seem as they actually are. There might be more to work with than at first appears. The problem you *think* you're trying to solve might not be the problem you *need* to solve.

Try bringing in a fresh set of eyes. Who knows? Maybe they'll see something you don't.

7. The Box Inside the Box

I once had a client who put so many restrictions on us creatively, I was convinced it was going to be pretty much impossible to do anything even remotely creative. At every turn it seemed like there was a roadblock of one kind or another. It was maddening.

And then, just as we were getting started on the project, our client called one day to say he had just gotten a job with another company. We were ecstatic, figuring that surely the new client that was coming in to replace him couldn't be any worse. Boy, were we ever wrong. She imposed even more limitations than the previous guy. Suddenly, our original limitations didn't seem all that bad by comparison.

What? You Thought There Wasn't Going to Be Homework?

175

From that experience I've since used this little exercise to put a particularly cramped conceptual environment into perspective. Here's what you do. Draw a three-by-three-inch square on a sheet of paper or whiteboard. Write as many ideas as you can fit inside the lines.

Now draw a six-by-six-inch square. Inside this larger square write down all the ideas you had in the first square and add as many new ones as you can fit. Finally, draw a twelve-by-twelve-inch square, writing down all the ideas in the six-inch square plus some even newer ones.

The twelve-inch square definitely has its limitations. But next to the three-inch square, it suddenly feels like you're working in the Astrodome. Try it. It works.

8. The Creative Alchemist

Sometimes you'll have an idea that in any other situation would be terrific. But because it lies outside the box, you have no choice but to reject it as being unworkable.

But maybe it's not. Try this. Again draw a box on a piece of paper. Label the box with the problem you're trying to solve. Let's say it's "create an intelligent lamp." Next draw a line down the middle of the box, dividing it into two sections, one on the left, one on the right. On the left side of the line, write "Ideas That Work." On the right side, write "Ideas That Don't."

Now let's say someone has an idea. Maybe it's "give the lamp a brain." Everyone gets a good chuckle, the idea goes down on the right side of the box, and that's that. Not a serious idea. It's off the table.

But wait a second. Could there be something here? What if the idea was tweaked a bit? Could the seemingly absurd idea of giving a lamp a brain be changed just enough to make it a good idea? Could you give the lamp an electronic brain? Could you put a tiny computer chip in it that records your patterns around the house, turning itself on and off accordingly? If the lamp knew that you like to watch TV with the lights on, it could automatically come on every time you turn the TV on.

Ideas aren't rigid things. They're malleable. They're organic. Sometimes all you need to do is turn your creative steering wheel a little to the left or right, and a seemingly unworkable idea can lead to a genuine breakthrough.

9. Wide-Angle Thinking

If you've ever heard the expression "You can't see the forest for the trees," you'll appreciate the idea behind this one. It's certainly true that there are times when you're just too close to the problem. Your view of it is just too narrow. That's when it makes sense to step back from the problem and take a wide-angle look at just what it is you're actually trying to accomplish.

I've been asking you to make a lot of boxes in this chapter. Well, why wouldn't I? If there weren't any boxes, there wouldn't be a Houdini Solution, right? So I'm going to ask you to draw yet another box, and again I'm going to ask you to state your creative goal inside the box. Let's pretend it's "design a faster sailboat."

What? You Thought There Wasn't Going to Be Homework?

177

To the right of the box, write down all the ideas you've already come up with. To the left of the box, make a new box and draw a line connecting it to the first one containing your creative goal, "design a faster sailboat."

Now inside the new box write down an even bigger creative goal for which the original goal now becomes its solution. In the sailboat example, maybe the new goal is: I want to get from Los Angeles to Hawaii more quickly.

You see what's happened? Now that the problem is wider, the first goal has now become a possible solution. But only one. What ideas might you come up with that could also get you from Los Angeles to Hawaii more quickly besides designing a faster sailboat? What about making the trip in a powerboat? A cruise ship would be faster. A 747 would be faster still. Maybe you could privately charter a Concorde. Sometimes it's easier to generate ideas against a bigger problem than a smaller one.

10. Finding the Metaphor

The science fiction author Ray Bradbury attributes much of his success to his ability to see metaphors in almost everything. *Fahrenheit 451*, for example, is a story about a dystopian future in which firemen start fires rather than put them out. At the same time, it's a metaphor for censorship and Big Brother.

As almost anyone in advertising will tell you, metaphors can help you solve a creative problem, too. Remember Prudential's Rock of Gibraltar? What better way to say solid than with a 1,400-foot-high slab of limestone.

How about Apple's "1984" TV commercial in which the young blonde girl hurls a sledgehammer at a gigantic screen on which a sinister face is extolling the virtues of compliance to the mindless masses gathered in the audience. The blonde, of course, represented the young upstart, Apple, smashing to smithereens the diabolical, mind-controlling IBM. Didn't exactly work out that way in the long run, but it was a great metaphor nonetheless.

You can use metaphors, too.

Start by clearly stating what it is you're trying to accomplish. Maybe it's "design the world's most unique hotel." Next make a list of metaphors—people, places, animals, actions, it can be almost anything—that are like your statement in some way. In this case, possible metaphors might be: anthill, Atlantis, tree house, igloo, hippie commune, space station.

Once that's done, pick one of your metaphors. Something interesting. Something as far away from the real problem as possible. And I mean really far away. In our example, how about tree house?

Now write a description of the metaphor you've chosen. Describe it physically. How big is it? Where is it usually found? What color is it? Also describe how it works. What effect does it have on things around it? How and where is it used?

A description of a tree house might include any of these: a series of platforms in a tree; can be reached by rope ladders; not found in cities; large tree required.

What? You Thought There Wasn't Going to Be Homework?

179

Finally, look at your description and see if you can find ideas that are relevant to your creative objective. Could a hotel be built in a tree? If not, could a restaurant in the hotel be located in a tree? Could the rooms be designed to feel like you're in a tree house?

Come up with as many ideas involving a tree house as you can. Then try one of the other metaphors on your list and see where that takes you.

11. Not-So-Free Association

Everyone knows about free association. You write down the problem, then you just let your consciousness go wild, writing down anything and everything that pops into your mind. It's a nonjudgmental technique, and it works beautifully in many situations.

But when you're thinking inside the box, and depending on just how small a box you're working in, free association isn't always the fastest way to get to a solution. While it definitely will generate a lot of ideas, many of those ideas are going to be completely unusable.

But what if free association weren't free at all? What if every idea that popped into your mind had a price tag on it? What if instead of just writing down anything and everything, you had to *pay* to write it down? You'd have to stop a second and ask yourself if an idea is literally worth writing down because just submitting it is going to cost you something.

Here's what to do. You'll need a bunch of poker chips, some magic markers, and a plastic bowl. Get everyone on the team together, and then divide the chips and the markers equally among them.

Next tell them you're going to do a modified version of free association, the only difference being that every time they have an idea or a thought they want to submit, they need to "pay" for it by putting one of their chips into the bowl.

Let's say Jim gets the ball rolling with Idea A. He writes an *A* on one of his chips and drops it in the bowl while the person running the session writes down Jim's idea and labels it "Idea A/Jim."

Keep doing this for as long as you want. Then have the group collectively evaluate each of the ideas, exploring the more interesting ones, seeing how many of them actually lead to something. Let's say it turns out to be Ideas A, J, L, M, R, and V.

Finally, empty the bowl and pull out the chips labeled A, J, L, M, R, and V. The people whose names are on the remaining chips have to spring for, say, beers for the entire team after work.

This is a great exercise that teaches people how to self-edit their creative thinking, submitting only ideas that they really feel good about. Again, if you've got time for conventional free association, do it. But when you're pressed for time and you need to streamline the creative process, go with not-so-free association every time.

12. Brutethink

This one comes from *Thinkertoys* author Michael Michalko. Basically, the idea is to force connections in a, well, brutish

What? You Thought There Wasn't Going to Be Homework?

181

way. What I like about Brutethink is that, because it forces you to shrink your creative mind-set into a ridiculously tight space, it has the effect of making your original box seem a lot less confining.

First write down the objective. Let's imagine it's "Create a new ice cream flavor."

Next get a dictionary. It could also be a newspaper, a magazine, a road atlas, a menu, a coffee cup sleeve, or anything else with words on it. Pick out a word. Don't put any thought into it. Just pick a word at random and write it down. Pretend the word is *moon*.

Make a list of as many word associations as you can that have anything whatsoever to do with your random word—in this case, moon. The list might include: planet, orbit, cheese, crater, Apollo, Armstrong, satellite, star, dust, glow, rocks, NASA, and Sea of Tranquility.

Next try coming up with as many connections between your random word and your stated objective as you can. In our example your list might include Moonilla, Moonberry, and Moonrocky Road.

Finally, make even more connections between the stated objective and the association words. In the moon example, you might have come up with OrbitIce, Starsoft, Space-Cream, and LemonDust.

13. Circling the Story

We all did this when we were kids. For me it was at summer camp. We'd all make a circle. Somebody would start making up a story. He'd suddenly stop, usually in midsentence. Then the kid next to him had to immediately jump in and keep the story going. Then he'd stop and the next kid would have to pick it up, and so on until it came back around to the first kid, where the story would finally end.

You can use a similar method to develop creative ideas.

The moderator starts it off by stating the problem. Maybe it's something like "Once upon a time there was a designer who wanted to design a radically different pair of binoculars, so he started by . . ." The person immediately to the moderator's right has to immediately pick up the story where the moderator leaves off. She might say, ". . . so he started by asking if there might be a way to install a tiny built-in video camera, which . . ." The next person in the circle seamlessly picks up the story from there: ". . . which didn't work because it weighed too much, so instead he . . ." Next person, ". . . so instead he invented a much smaller camera that held only three minutes of footage . . ."

On it goes until the story has gone all the way around the circle at least once, although if it's really going well, you can just keep it going around and around for as long as you like.

I really like this technique a lot. For one thing, because each person in the circle has to pick up the story immediately and without hesitation, it tends to rely strongly on the subconscious. Because no one has time to think much, this tends to put a damper on chronically negative people, who usually need at least a few seconds to think up a reason why an idea won't work.

That's not to say that a patently ill-conceived idea won't get weeded out or reshaped into a great idea. As you can see in the example, the first pass at an integral video camera was accepted as a good idea but not in its original form.

What? You Thought There Wasn't Going to Be Homework?

183

14. Go in Through the Back Door

There are times when no matter how hard you try to keep the creative process moving forward, you can't. So don't. Instead, tell the team that you're going to solve the problem by going in through the back door.

In effect, you're going to think from the opposite, or reverse, direction. By coming in through the back door, you get to see an alternative angle of attack—how your counterparts in, say, some alternative reality system might come at the problem.

Let's pick a really straightforward objective: "How can I become wealthy?" But when you go in through the back door, the problem suddenly becomes this: "How can I keep from becoming dirt poor?"

What are all the things that could make you poor? Is there a big customer that, if he were to take his business somewhere else, might cripple your company? Could the market for your product suddenly go south? Is your company financially sound enough to absorb a cataclysmic blow to the economy, such as a major terrorist attack?

Interestingly, the solutions you come up with for the back-door problem almost always lead you to solutions for the front-door version.

15. Storyboarding

A lot of advertising agencies present TV ideas using what's called a ripomatic, which is essentially a rough TV commercial using actual film clips "ripped" from movies, TV shows, music videos, and basically any other kind of available footage.

But the storyboard is still an effective way to map out the sequence of events, the plot points, in a commercial. Essentially, it's just a series of boxes with key visuals, beneath which are lettered dialogue, sound effects, and camera instructions.

Because Walt Disney was frequently working with hundreds and sometimes thousands of drawings, he used storyboarding as a way to keep track of them all by having his animators pin their work, frame by frame, onto a wall, making it easy to decide which scenes should stay and which should be discarded.

Storyboarding is a great way to concept ideas, too. It lets you visualize the scope of the project. It lets you keep the group on track by avoiding unfocused discussion. And it lets you easily identify and organize your ideas.

When you storyboard you start to see connections. You begin to see how one idea relates to the others and how they all come together. And because everyone's ideas are up on a wall, there's a greater tendency for people to get more deeply immersed in the project.

16. Down the Rabbit Hole

Never let it be said that *Alice in Wonderland* creator Lewis Carroll didn't have a wildly spectacular imagination. He wrote the following little puzzle. See if you can solve it.

What? You Thought There Wasn't Going to Be Homework?

185

John gave his brother James a box:
About it there were many locks.
James woke and said it gave him pain;
So gave it back to John again.
The box was not with lid supplied
Yet caused two lids to open wide:
And all these locks had never a key
What kind of box, then, could it be?[1]

17. The Sand Box

I put before you six boxes. The first three are filled with sand. The other three are empty. Your task? Arrange the six boxes so that no full box of sand is next to an empty box. No empty box can be next to another empty box. Oh, yeah, I forgot. You can only move one box at a time. So here's what I want to know. How many moves did it take you to solve the problem? The fewer the better.[2]

18. Is It or Isn't It?

As we've learned already, sometimes what we see as limitations really aren't limitations at all. And if they are, maybe they aren't quite as restricting as we've been led to believe. This is an important thing to know, of course, because we need all the thinking space we can get when we're thinking inside the box. Here's a good way to see just how limiting your limits are:

1. State the objective. (Example: I want to make my restaurant more appealing.)

2. Next think up some two-sides-of-the-same-coin strategic ideas that are relevant to the problem. (Examples: expand/not expand, food is boring/new menu selections, main dining room is too small/main dining room is cozy.)

3. Choose just one of your strategic sets that, for whatever reason, seems to resonate with you. (Let's assume it's food is boring/new menu selections.)

4. Identify firm examples of each pole from your area of concern. (Example: "We've had the same chef for seventeen years" versus "We've recently added several new international entrées.")

5. Now see if you can rephrase each side of the coin so that your evaluation is reversed but still true. (Example: another way of saying "We've had the same chef for seventeen years" might be "We've had tremendous stability in the kitchen.")

19. Word Racing

This is a simple little word game that my wife first introduced me to, although I often wish she hadn't because I think I've actually beaten her at it maybe once. But I've got to admit, it really does show you how creative you can be when the clock is ticking.

Give each person on the team a sheet of paper and a pencil. Come up with a short phrase. At first, keep it really short. Something like, say, Boston Red Sox. Each person

What? You Thought There Wasn't Going to Be Homework?

187

gets five minutes to make as many words as he or she can think of using only the letters found in the phrase.

For Boston Red Sox, some words might be: bore, rex, stone, and store. Trust me, there are dozens more. Keep in mind that if a letter only appears once, you can only use it once. If it appears twice, you can use it twice. For instance, "rooster" doesn't qualify because there's only one *r* in "Boston Red Sox."

When the five minutes are up, everyone stops and counts their words. Whoever has the most words wins. Then comes the fun part. Try the game again, only this time make the phrase longer and the time limit shorter.

20. Dr. Livingstone, I Assume

As I pointed out in Chapter 8, we come into this world with an open mind. But then, as we grow older, our thinking becomes more structured, even rigid. Horses can't have horns growing out of their heads. Sand can't be purple. Stars are too high to touch.

As our thinking becomes more structured, we start to assume things. Rain is always wet. Snow is white. If I step on the gas pedal, I will go faster. If I go into a restaurant, there will be food.

Most of the time our assumptions are accurate. But when we're trying to innovate, either inside or outside the box, it's important that we learn to suspend assumptions. When we do we're free to sail off into all kinds of directions, one or more of which might lead us to something new and wonderful.

In his book *Test Your Lateral Thinking IQ*, Paul Sloan tells the story of the Maginot Line, the fortification along the Franco-German border, built by the French to protect their country against an invasion by the Germans. The French assumed that the next war would be fought the same way as the last. But as they discovered when the German blitzkrieg came through Belgium into France, it was obvious that that assumption had been wrong.

Creativity guru Edward de Bono has a great exercise that can help challenge this kind of assumption blindness using provocative statements that go out of their way to slap down the assumption.

Let's say you want to develop a new concept in delivering packages. Start by listing some assumptions about package delivery. One of them might be that "it takes an average of three to five days to deliver a package."

Now turn the assumption into a provocation. Instead of the assumption that "it takes an average of three to five days to deliver a package," the provocation becomes "a package can be delivered overnight." Using the provocation as an escape hatch, you can now start thinking about shipping in a new way. Former crop-dusting pilot Fred Smith did exactly that, and the result was Federal Express.

21. Are We There Yet?

Anyone who has kids knows that age when all they ever ask is "why?"

Why did we get a new car? Because our old car was getting old.

What? You Thought There Wasn't Going to Be Homework?

189

Why? Because we drove it a lot.

Why? Because we needed to go to work.

Why? Because we needed to make money.

Why? Because we need money to pay for things.

And on and on and on it can go.

As it turns out, asking "why?" turns out to be a good way to get to the core of a problem and with any luck a good creative solution.

> Asking "why?" turns out to be a good way to get to the core of a problem and with any luck a good creative solution.

22. Creative Magnetism

Once upon a time, a guy by the name of Dave Katell was suffering from writer's block. He thought it might help if he wrote down interesting words on pieces of paper and then rearranged them, hoping they might inspire him. Eventually, the pieces of paper became small magnets that he would stick on his refrigerator door. Word got around, and pretty soon Magnetic Poetry was born.

What Dave didn't know is that his word magnets can also be a pretty fun way to come up with ideas. You can do this exercise using the words from a magnetic poetry set. Or you can get yourself a stack of 3″ × 5″ index cards. Pull out a dictionary and randomly pick out a word and write it down on one of the cards. Do this for the entire stack. When you're finished, spread all the cards out on a table. Think about the problem you're trying to solve. Then let your eyes wander over the cards. See if a word feels like it's in some way relevant. It doesn't matter what the word is. It doesn't matter if it's literally relevant or not. It just has to *feel* right. Keep doing this until you've pulled out a dozen cards. Now assemble the twelve cards in different orders and see if they drive you toward an idea. They almost always will.

23. Out of Your Mind

Who we are has everything to do with our past, what schools we attended, who our friends were, and so many other factors that make us unique and give us our own special outlook on life.

That's great except sometimes that very uniqueness can get us stuck inside ourselves, preventing us from seeing innovative solutions to problems.

What if you could get out of yourself for a while? What if you could slip inside someone else's brain and think the way he or she does? Because you'd see things differently, chances are your approach to solving problems would be different, too.

Needless to say, we can't literally jump in and out of other people's brains. But we can do the next best thing. We can imagine what it's like to be someone else.

Try this. On a piece of paper or on a whiteboard, state the problem the team is trying to solve. For example, "How can we create a whole new concept in minivans?"

Next have each person on the team write down the name of someone they consider to be creative. It can be anyone from Steven Spielberg to their eighty-five-year-old grand-

What? You Thought There Wasn't Going to Be Homework?

191

mother, as long as it's someone they are familiar with and admire for their creative ability.

Under the name, have them write a "What Would It Be Like" statement. So if someone chooses, say, Aaron Sorkin, the creator of "The West Wing," they'd write, "If Aaron Sorkin created a new kind of minivan, what would it be like?" Give everyone twenty minutes to come up with a list of at least ten things. In our Aaron Sorkin minivan example, you might have any of these responses: "It would make an otherwise boring vehicle actually seem exciting." "It would have a lot of different features (subplots) that all tie together seamlessly." "The design would force you to pay attention." "It would constantly surprise you." "It would assume you are an intelligent person."

Finally, have everyone share their lists. See if there are some common themes. There will be. Focus on those.

24. What Is It?

Whoever makes it, tells it not. Whoever takes it, knows it not. And whoever knows it, wants it not. What is it?[3]

25. Bottles and Knives

I love this exercise from Edward de Bono's book *The Five-Day Course in Thinking*. As far as I'm concerned, it's custom-tailored for the Houdini Solution. It has tight limitations. When you first ponder it, like any problem where you're trying to think inside the box, it seems impossible to solve. But it's not.

Visualize three narrow-necked soda bottles and four table knives. Place the three bottles upright on a table so that each bottle forms the corner of a triangle. The distance between the bases of any two bottles should be slightly more than the length of a knife.

Using the knives, construct a platform on top of the three bottles. No part of any knife may touch the table. The platform has to be strong enough to support a full glass of water.[4]

26. Run for Your Life

Say you're Dr. Richard Kimble. You've been falsely accused of killing your wife. You've been on the run ever since, trying to stay one step ahead of Lieutenant Philip Gerard, the relentless detective who's been dogging you for years. One night you decide to go see a movie. There you are, munching your buttered popcorn, when Gerard and several police officers enter the theater. At first you panic. They've got all the exits covered. It's only a matter of time before they find you. Then you remember the Houdini Solution. If you think inside the box, you can escape. But how?[5]

27. Where There's Gold, There's Usually More Gold

It really is true. A good idea is worth its weight in gold. And just like when a prospector finds a single nugget, you've got to figure there's a deeper vein hidden, lurking somewhere nearby. All you have to do is snoop around a little. This exercise will help make the snooping easier.

What? You Thought There Wasn't Going to Be Homework?

193

Draw a box in the middle of a sheet of a paper. Inside the box state the problem.

Next, using one or more of the techniques in this chapter, brainstorm ideas. Don't even think about leaving the room until you've generated at least six creative, and potentially workable, solutions. Write each solution in another box outside the first box.

Think you've got a few golden nuggets there? Great. But now let's see if there's more where those came from.

Let's say you've come up with eight solutions to the central problem that everyone feels pretty good about. On eight separate sheets of paper, draw a new box, and inside it write one of the eight solutions.

Now, just like you did in the first round, brainstorm as many new ideas off of that one idea as you can. Do this for all eight first-round nuggets.

If you're up for it, you can keep this little mining expedition going for as long as it keeps generating good ideas. Sometimes you hit pay dirt near the surface. Sometimes you hit it deeper down.

The point is, sometimes you have to dig for a big idea. Not always, of course. Sometimes it can smack you in the brain like a thirty-pound sledgehammer. That happens. But a lot of the time, you've got to play the miner. You've got to dig.

28. Learning to Think Inside the Box, Priceless

Few ideas in advertising have held up as well as Master-Card's "Priceless" campaign. From its launch in October of

1997, the campaign has evolved to become a case study in successful global advertising. Having earned every major creative award in the industry and more than a hundred individual awards, "Priceless" has routinely been heralded as one of the most successful campaigns ever created.

When you're a creative guy in an ad agency, you will often inherit an existing campaign like MasterCard's and, working within its already-established creative boundaries, will have to find new ways to keep the idea fresh and memorable.

Let's pretend that's you. I've just called you into my office. I want you to work on MasterCard. You already know the drill. Something something, $25. Something something, $187. Something something, priceless. Easy, right?

Oh, one other thing. Before I brought you on, the last team had already come up with a storyline and the client really digs it. In other words, the box just got even smaller.

OK, here's the commercial. You fill in the blanks.

Open on a gorgeous yacht lying at anchor on a sun-drenched lagoon. A man is standing on the bow. _____: $52. We see another man rowing out to the yacht. _____ and _____: $129. The man in the rowboat comes alongside the yacht and hands the other man an envelope. _____: $40. The man opens the envelope. He pulls out a letter. He reads it. A big grin sweeps over his face. _____: priceless. Finally, we see the man dive into the lagoon. Obviously, whatever was in the letter has made him very happy.

How did you do? This is one of two actual MasterCard commercials that were created as part of a consumer promotion where ordinary people just like you were given a

What? You Thought There Wasn't Going to Be Homework?

195

chance to fill in these same blanks. Unlike you, the winner's creation was seen by millions of people on national television.

29. Walk the Line

No, you don't have to dress like Johnny Cash and take guitar lessons. Get yourself a pencil and place the point in the middle of a piece of paper. What I want you to do is draw a picture of something that symbolizes the problem you're trying to solve.

For example, if you own a chain of pizza shops and you're trying to come up with a way to decrease your delivery times, you could draw a clock or a pizza or how about a pizza with an hour hand and a minute hand. Don't worry if you don't draw very well. That doesn't matter. *What does matter is that you never lift your pencil off the paper.* That's right. Once you start drawing, the point of your pencil must stay in contact with the paper at all times until you're finished. Try it a few times. Most people find this pretty hard to do at first, but after a few tries it gets increasingly easier. Until I ask you to do this . . .

30. Walk the Line Backward

Same as above. But with your opposite hand.

31. Walk the Line Backward in the Dark

Same as above. But with your eyes closed.

32. Somebody Just Shoot Me

Teaching yourself how to think visually within creative boundaries can have a huge payoff everywhere else. So here's another great visual exercise that will literally change how you see the world around you.

As always, state your creative problem. So maybe you run Fender Guitars and you want to design a radically new kind of electric guitar. Now go find a still camera. Doesn't matter if it's digital or film. Next go find something that more or less personifies the problem. Because a conventional guitar seems like an obvious place to start, take a picture of the guitar.

But don't stop there. Find other things that make you think of guitars. Competitors' guitars, maybe. Take pictures of those, too. Now shoot pictures of people playing guitars. And so forth. Once you've got lots of pictures, pin them up on a wall. Upside down. Do you see anything different? Is there a shape or a curve that could lead to something new and different?

33. SCAMPER

Even if you don't work in advertising, there's a good chance you've heard of the ad agency BBDO. And if you haven't—well, you've definitely seen its work. BBDO has probably done more award-winning Super Bowl commercials than anyone else in the business.

This exercise was invented by the *O* in BBDO. That would be Fred Osborne. Among other things, Osborne is

What? You Thought There Wasn't Going to Be Homework?

197

widely credited as being the father of brainstorming. A long time ago he invented a technique he called SCAMPER.

It's based on the premise that there really are no new ideas, only mutated versions of existing ones. As creative techniques go, SCAMPER has proven to be a pretty sticky idea. I can understand why. So will you once you try it.

SCAMPER, if you haven't guessed already, is an acronym. It stands for *S*ubstitute, *C*ombine, *A*dapt, *M*odify, *P*ut to other uses, *E*liminate, and *R*earrange.

Because SCAMPER is about action, it doesn't just get you to think about solutions—it actually guides you toward them by forcing you to look at the problem in specific ways.

Let's start by explaining what each word means and what it's trying to achieve in a general sense, and then we'll get into how the technique might work against a real objective.

Substitute. What can I substitute for what's here now? What can I use instead? Could other materials work? Is there another route I could take? Is there another color? Is there another location? Is there different music?

Combine. What can I combine or bring together somehow? Would this go with that? Is there a way I can combine something with something else? Could I marry this objective with that one? If I join this department and that department, what might happen?

Adapt. Is there a way I can adapt a solution that's already in place? What else is like this? Is there something from the past that could work for me now? Is there another idea that's been used for something else that I could make my own?

Modify. Can I change something that would create something new? Can I make something a different color? What about a different shape, a different sound, a different smell? What can I add? Can I make it stronger? Heavier? Lighter? Can I make it bigger? Can I remove something? What happens if I make this smaller?

Put to other uses. Is there something else I could use this for? Is there a way to use it that I'm not seeing? If I changed it somehow, could it be used for something else?

Eliminate. What could I eliminate? If I took something away, how would that change this? Could I cut the cost? What would happen if I reduced the number of colors? If I made it smaller? If I made it easier to understand? If it weren't as loud?

Rearrange. What could I rearrange in some way? What would happen if I switched things around? What if my background became my foreground and my foreground became my background? Is there another order in which this process could unfold? What if I made the effect of a cause the cause itself? If

What? You Thought There Wasn't Going to Be Homework?

199

the things we do fast were slowed down, what would that do? If the things we do slowly were speeded up, what would happen?

OK, so let's see how SCAMPER might work in a real-world situation. Here's the challenge: I want to invent a new type of kite.

Substitute. Could the tail of the kite be made of something else? What about plastic? What about aluminum foil? What about denim? What if instead of string, I use ultrathin fiber-optic cable that could light up at night?

Combine. Could the kite double as a decorative piece in my home? Could I combine it with a little electric motor to help it go even higher? Could I coat the fabric with something that would make the wind slip more easily over it?

Adapt. How can I adapt the kite? Can I change its shape? Could it be octagonal? A rhombus? Could it be shaped like an animal? Or a battleship? Or a comet? Could I put a tiny camera mount on the frame?

Modify. Can I modify the kite in some way? Can I make it transparent? Can I make it hum as air passes over it? What if I made the kite out of material that glows in the dark?

Put to other uses. What could a kite be besides a kite? Could it be an advertising medium? Could I sell space on it? If I put a big "SOS" on it, could lost hikers use it to attract rescue crews?

Eliminate. Could I get rid of something that would make the kite better? What if by getting rid of the string, I could control the kite with a radio control transmitter? If it were lighter, would it fly better?

Rearrange. What if the tail were on top and the kite itself were on the bottom? What would happen if I put the frame inside the kite instead of outside?

34. The Fact Matrix

In the movie *The Matrix*, a young computer programmer named Anderson discovers from his mentor, Morpheus, that the world Anderson believes to be real is, in fact, nothing but an illusion created by machines bent on controlling the human race. In a way, we sometimes live in the Matrix, too. I call it The Fact Matrix.

The truth is, much of the time we either accept things as facts too quickly or cling to that acceptance for too long. This can be a problem because facts, no matter how seemingly irrefutable they might appear, have a way of changing over time. For generations we had every reason to believe the sun revolved around the earth. And we might still, if Copernicus hadn't come along and said, "Well, I don't think so."

As I've said already, if you're going to think inside the box effectively, you've got to be able to challenge what you

What? You Thought There Wasn't Going to Be Homework?

201

believe the box is made of. Just because you think Wall A lies here doesn't mean Wall A actually does. Sure, it might have at one time. But circumstances, like wind on a beach, can and do shift things around over time. What might have been cast in stone once could have changed right under your nose, and you'd never know it.

The Fact Matrix Challenge can help you take a hard look at the facts as you know them and hopefully get you to see them as they really are.

Here's how it works.

First list a fact that you believe defines the problem you're trying to solve. I'll call this a Mr. Anderson fact. Next to each Mr. Anderson fact, write a statement that challenges it. Let's call this a Morpheus fact. Don't hold back. Don't be judgmental. Just write it down. Finally, think about the Morpheus fact. Brainstorm it. What new ideas does it suggest to you?

Example

1. **Mr. Anderson fact:** All car tires go flat when punctured by a nail.
2. **Morpheus fact:** All car tires run even when punctured by a nail.
3. **New idea:** Apply to the inner lining of all car tires a self-sealing coating that heals punctures instantly.

Fill in the Blanks

1. **Mr. Anderson fact:** Insurance rates are based on actuarial tables.

2. Morpheus fact: _____

_____

3. New idea: _____

_____

1. **Mr. Anderson fact:** Doughnuts are made of dough.

2. Morpheus fact: _____

_____

3. New idea: _____

_____

1. **Mr. Anderson fact:** Coffee is brown.

2. Morpheus fact: _____

_____

3. New idea: _____

_____

35. Back to the Future

There's a technique in Buddhism called Remembrance. The idea is that you can induce new states of mind by remembering something that, in fact, has not yet happened.

What? You Thought There Wasn't Going to Be Homework?

203

Think about your problem. Spend some time with it. Look at it from several angles.

Now imagine it's already been solved at some point in the past. Think about what your company would be like now if it had. Where would you be? How would the solution have changed the organization?

Invent some memories. What do you remember happening at the moment the problem was solved? What did it feel like? What went through your mind? Write it all down.

Imagine you're a witness in a trial and you've been asked to remember in as much detail as you can what happened that day. How would you do that? How would you dig back in your memory banks and recall what happened?

Use your senses. Where did it happen? At the office? Whose office? Yours? Someone else's? What did the room look like? Do you remember something someone said? What was the weather like that day? What were you wearing?

What you're trying to do is trick your subconscious into believing that something has actually happened when in truth it hasn't. While it sounds hard to do, it isn't.

The mind has a way of being exceptionally conducive to manufacturing false memories and making them seem extremely vivid and real, as any psychologist who's ever worked with people who've claimed to have been abducted by aliens will tell you.

Sometimes the easiest way to imagine solving something is by imagining you already have.

36. Night of the Knightless

If there's an official game of the Houdini Solution, it's chess. Not only does chess challenge you to think strategically, it challenges you to think creatively using pieces that have limitations on how they can move around the board.

For example, pawns can only move forward, bishops can only move diagonally, the king can only move one square at a time.

While I'm no Bobby Fischer, I know enough about chess to realize that the top players are incredibly creative people.

Think about it. The chess world didn't call it the Ponziani opening just because people thought Domenico Lorenzo Ponziani was a nice guy. They called it that because he's the guy who invented it.

> Chess is a great way to develop your thinking-inside-the-box creativity.

So chess is a great way to develop your thinking-inside-the-box creativity.

But what happens when you take away some of your weapons? What happens when you make the box smaller? The game gets a lot harder. The walls between you and winning suddenly get a lot higher and a lot more creatively challenging.

To start, try playing a game without your knights. Then try another game without your bishops or your queen. Keep taking away pieces, making it harder and harder for yourself. A great player could probably beat both of us with nothing but pawns. I can't. And chances are, neither can you. It doesn't matter. The mere act of forcing your mind

What? You Thought There Wasn't Going to Be Homework?

205

to work around a self-inflicted handicap like this will get you thinking differently.

And if you don't play chess, not a problem. The exercise works with a lot of different games. If you like poker, try dealing yourself only three cards to everyone else's five. Even Monopoly works. Instead of starting with $1,500, start with $500.

37. Kill the Babies

As anyone in advertising can tell you, it's easy to fall in love with an idea. And you know when you've stumbled onto a great one. A big smile comes over your face. Something just goes click, and you know it's a winner.

But what happens when your baby gets poked in the eye by the client?

At that point, you've got three choices: (1) you can curl up on the conference room floor with your thumb in your mouth and make unintelligible gurgling noises, (2) you can throw your half-empty Starbucks cup at the client, or (3) you can show a little resiliency.

From personal experience, I'm going to suggest you go with the third option.

But even better, why not prevent yourself from ever getting in that position in the first place. We all get excited when we come up with a huge idea. But there can be any number of reasons why it can't or simply won't ever see the light of day. So while it's great to hit on a great big, monstrous, pump-fisting idea, you've got to teach yourself that as wonderful a solution as it is, it's not the only wonderful solution.

As you try the different techniques in this chapter, you're going to uncover big, inside-the-box ideas, one or more of which you're going to be convinced is *the solution*. But when that idea does surface, put it aside and pretend it's been shot down. How does that make you feel? It's OK to feel frustrated. It's OK to be disappointed. But it's not OK to feel no other idea will ever be as good as *the idea*.

Kill your baby and keep going. The great creative people are unbelievably resilient.

38. Let It Go

A man is holding a block of wood. If he lets it go, what will happen?[6]

39. Shape World

In this exercise, you'll learn to overcome your own ingrained biases by working with common shapes that you've lived with all your life—each of which has an unmistakable meaning.

First create a scene using pictures cut out from magazines and newspapers. Make sure there are people in your scene. Roads and buildings, too. Maybe it's a small town. Or the block your company is located on.

Now make three shapes: (1) a red hexagon, (2) a circle with a diagonal line cutting through it, and (3) a thought bubble like the ones in comic strips. Make several copies of each shape.

What? You Thought There Wasn't Going to Be Homework?

207

Start by asking the team members to place each shape in the scene where they think it belongs. At an intersection they'd place the red hexagon. The thought bubbles would go next to people. The circles with the diagonal lines might go next to a frozen pond or a construction site.

Now tell everyone that they've just crossed into an alternate universe, a parallel dimension. The scene is the same. But this time the meaning in the shapes get mixed up. The red hexagon becomes the thought bubble, the thought bubble becomes the circle with the diagonal line, and the circle with the diagonal line becomes the red hexagon.

Try the exercise again.

At first it might feel kind of strange seeing a person's "thoughts" represented by a red hexagon, for example, but it's surprising how quickly this new reality begins to feel totally natural.

40. Speed TV

In advertising you get used to getting a message out in thirty seconds. Sometimes in fifteen. And lately even five. Most people find this incredibly difficult to do. I've bid commercials out to feature film directors who have told me they don't do commercials precisely because they found it impossible to work in such a minuscule window of time.

But again I will say it. There is no better way to force you to go directly to the core of a solution than the limitation of time.

To prove this to yourself, take one of the ideas you've generated. Now write a thirty-second radio script that conveys the idea. Don't worry if your commercial isn't exactly award-winning. Just get the essence of your idea out in thirty seconds in a way that's inspiring, engaging, and compelling.

Now try it in fifteen seconds.

Finally, shrink it down to five.

If you can convince somebody in five seconds of anything, trust me—you do indeed have a great idea.

41. The Coldest Day

Describe the coldest day you can remember without using any of these words: cold, temperature, thermometer, snow, icy, ice, frozen, freeze, biting, plunge, mercury, bitter, snap, wind, winter, shiver, goose bumps, gloves, mittens, wool, hat, boots, scarf, snowman, chill, chilly, frost, or frosty.

42. Poetry Jam

You might not think so, but some of the greatest poetry really does depend a lot on structure. For my money few people are as good at thinking inside the box as poets.

In this exercise I'm going to ask you to write a poem. No one is expecting you to be the second coming of Shelley or Yeats. The important thing is to make the poem adhere to the following rules:

1. The first line has to involve an emotion: sadness, fear, joy—whatever you feel.

What? You Thought There Wasn't Going to Be Homework?

209

2. The second line has to describe the emotion as a color. For example, anger might be "red as a fire truck." Fear might be "black as coal."
3. The third line has to begin with "_____ happens when . . ." For example, "Anger happens when the dog throws up on the couch" or "Fear happens when I'm in the dark."
4. The fourth line has to begin with "_____ sounds like . . ." For example, "Confusion sounds like trees swishing in the wind."
5. Finally, the last line of the poem has to repeat the emotion in the first line.

43. What Would Kojak Have Done?

There's been a murder. Two bodies lie in a puddle of water in a room. Broken glass is everywhere. Through an open window, a cat can be seen running off into the distance. What happened?[7]

44. Dream Sequence

For years, Sam Hawks had been night watchman at the Phoenixville National Bank. He was well liked for the way he faithfully performed his duties and for his cheerful manner.

One night, Mr. Stuart, the president of the bank, came in at eight o'clock. He greeted old Sam and explained to him that he was going in to get some papers from his office. He'd been called to the city, he said, and planned to catch a ten o'clock flight.

As Sam listened an anxious look came over his face. "Don't take that plane, Mr. Stuart," he said earnestly.

"Why not, Sam?" asked the banker, touched by the old fellow's sincerity and obvious distress. "Why not? What do you mean?"

"Mr. Stuart," Sam said, "I had a dream about that plane last night. I saw it crash to earth, and all the people aboard were killed. There was a terrible explosion and—oh, it was awful!" The poor man was almost in tears.

The bank president patted his arm and said, "Thank you, Sam. I'll see about it." And then he proceeded into the bank to get his papers.

Despite Sam's warning, Mr. Stuart did take the plane, and you'll be relieved to know, there was no accident.

When he returned to Phoenixville, the bank president's first action was to fire Sam. Why?[8]

45. The Heir Not So Apparent

At the end of World War II, the few scattered members of a once-rich and important Central European family who had survived concentration camps managed to come together.

The family fortune, although much diminished, was still of considerable size. In due course these few known survivors died, and the courts began a search for a possible heir to the estate.

Two candidates showed up, both claiming to be the same person—the only son of the last head of the family. Their stories were similar. Both claimed to have been in slave-labor camps. Both provided the same information on the

What? You Thought There Wasn't Going to Be Homework?

211

family history. Both had a superficial resemblance between them. The old acquaintances could not decide which was the true heir.

The magistrate in charge of the case decided to interview them separately. To the first candidate, the magistrate proposed a simple identity test. When the man readily agreed, the magistrate immediately said, "Arrest this man! He's an impostor! The other is the true heir." How could the magistrate have known this?[9]

46. A Bridge Too Far

Pete Tyler was walking home from the market with three cantaloupes. On the footbridge that he had to cross, there was a sign. It said the bridge's capacity was two hundred pounds. Peter himself weighed one hundred ninety-six pounds, and he knew the cantaloupes each weighed two pounds. He could make two trips, he thought. That would work. But then he had an idea that would let him and the cantaloupes make it across the bridge safely in one trip. How did he do it?[10]

47. Kipling's Dominoes

Rudyard Kipling wrote *The Jungle Book* and *The Light That Failed*. He also wrote this:

> *I have six honest serving men*
> *They taught me all I knew*
> *I call them What and Where and When*
> *And How and Why and Who.*

I call this Kipling's Dominoes because it involves asking a series of questions that follow in a sequential order:

1. What is the problem?
2. Where is it happening?
3. When is it happening?
4. Why is it happening?
5. How can I overcome the problem?
6. Who needs to be involved?
7. How will I know the problem is solved?

Here's how a typical Kipling Domino sequence might go:

1. What is the problem? (My briefcase is too heavy.)
2. Where is it happening? (At the train station.)
3. When is it happening? (When I go to the bookstore.)
4. Why is it happening? (Because I buy too many books.)
5. How can I overcome the problem? (Order the books online.)
6. Who needs to be involved? (The bookstore's website.)
7. How will I know the problem is solved? (When my briefcase is lighter.)

48. The Other Da Vinci Code

You might think that one of the greatest painters of all time would have been a pretty spontaneous guy, just sort of

What? You Thought There Wasn't Going to Be Homework?

213

painting whatever came to him in any given moment. But as it turns out, there was a method to Leonardo da Vinci's genius.

Da Vinci was a great one for collecting details. He was a keen observer, and he kept records of everything. He didn't just see noses, for instance. He saw hooked noses or bulbous noses or aquiline noses. He didn't just see eyes. He saw almond-shaped eyes. Soft eyes. Penetrating eyes. Sad eyes. Curious eyes.

Logically, most if not all of these physical attributes easily fell into a category: nose shape, eye shape, hair, muscular structure, foot shape—the list was long. By combining different attributes from different categories, Leonardo had virtually endless ways in which he could imagine his subject, and, in fact, this might well have been the manner in which he conceived the *Mona Lisa.*

Here's the kind of category/attribute grid that Leonardo da Vinci might have worked with:

Nose	Eyes	Mouth	Ears
hooked	circular	severe	pointy
pudgy	almond	droopy	small
wide	beady	puffy	elephantine
turned up	suspicious	pouty	narrow

Even this list, short as it is, offers the possibility for hundreds of potential combinations. A face could have a hooked nose, beady eyes, a pouty mouth, and small ears. Another face could have a wide nose, circular eyes, a droopy mouth, and pointy ears.

You can use da Vinci's technique to come up with your own *Mona Lisa*. Here's how:

1. Specify the challenge.
2. Next decide on your categories. They can be anything you want, and there can be as many of them as you think are necessary. Write them across the top of a sheet of paper.
3. Under each category write down as many attributes as you like. The more categories and attributes you have, the more opportunities for ideas will be generated. A grid with ten categories with ten attributes each means you'll end up with ten billion ideas.
4. When you're done connect one attribute from each category, creating a unique combination and hopefully a usable idea. Keep it random. Don't try to engineer the combinations as you go. Just pick an attribute, connect it with one in the next category, connect that with one in the next category, and so forth.

Here's an example to get you started. You own a bakery and want to come up with an idea for extending your brand into a new market.

You decide to focus on four categories: "What I Bake," "Fruits," "Nuts," and "Miscellaneous." Now make your grid, listing your four categories across the top, and then list your attributes under each category. Maybe it looks like this:

What? You Thought There Wasn't Going to Be Homework?

215

What I Bake	Fruits	Nuts	Miscellaneous
pies	orange	walnut	oatmeal
cakes	apple	almond	whipped cream
tarts	banana	cashew	granola
buns	blueberry	peanut	raisins
rolls	strawberry	macadamia	chocolate
bread	raspberry	hazelnut	pudding

Try making some connections of your own. See how many interesting ideas you can come up with.

49. Journey to the Center of the Idea

When you're stuck in an office, it can be hard to get inspired. Looking at the same walls day in and day out can sometimes dampen your ability to unplug from the routine and let your mind wander off into new territory.

What might work is to take everyone on the team on a little journey.

First pick a destination. Let's say it's the Mojave Desert. Ask everyone to spend ten to fifteen minutes writing down what they see and experience out there. What they encounter. Who they encounter. What the sky looks like. What it smells like. What sounds they hear. What the colors are like.

When everyone is finished have each person read his or her list out loud and then hang it up on the wall. When everyone's list is on the wall, see if anything spurs an idea.

This is, in fact, how the Sidewinder missile was created. A bunch of weapons designers were trying to find new ways to modify air-to-air guided missiles. They went on a virtual journey in the desert. Someone wrote down "sidewinder snake," someone else mentioned that the sidewinder hunts its prey by sensing its body heat, and just like that the Sidewinder missile was created.

50. The Five Houses of Einstein

They say Albert Einstein came up with this one. There are five houses in five different colors. In each house lives a person of a different nationality. The five owners drink a certain type of beverage, smoke a certain brand of cigar, and keep a certain kind of pet. Using the following clues, can you determine who owns the fish?

The Brit lives in a red house.

The Swede keeps dogs as pets.

The Dane drinks tea.

The green house is on the immediate left of the white house.

The green house owner drinks coffee.

The person who smokes Pall Mall rears birds.

The owner of the yellow house smokes Dunhill.

The man living in the house right in the middle drinks milk.

The Norwegian lives in the first house.

What? You Thought There Wasn't Going to Be Homework?

217

The man who smokes Blend lives next door to the one who keeps cats.

The man who keeps horses lives next door to the man who smokes Dunhill.

The owner who smokes Blue Master drinks beer.

The German smokes Prince.

The Norwegian lives next to the blue house.

The man who smokes Blend has a neighbor who drinks water.[11]

And the Walls Came a-Tumblin' Down; Is That a Good Thing?

I hope you can see by now that it's not. Barriers are essential to purposeful creativity. I hope I've shown you that it's only when our creative selves are confronted with limitations that we're able to give birth to truly great ideas. Sometimes big. Sometimes small. But always brilliant. And always in a way that can change your company, and your life, for the better.

Answers

[1]As curly haired James was sleeping in bed,
His brother John gave him a blow on the head.
James opened his eyelids, and spying his brother,
Doubled his fists, and gave him another.
This kind of a box then is not so rare
The lids are the eyelids, the locks are the hair.

[2]The problem can be solved by moving one box. Here's how. Just pick up the middle box filled with sand, pour the sand into the middle empty box, then put the box back where it was.

[3] Counterfeit money.

[4] With the handles of the three knives lying atop the bottles, arrange the blades of the knives so that they overlap. "But wait a minute," you say. "You said there were four knives." That's right, I did. But I didn't say you had to use them.

[5] You jump up and yell, "Fire!" Pandemonium ensues. Everyone jumps up and rushes for the exits. You easily escape amid the confusion. Do not try this at home. And definitely do not do this in an actual movie theater.

[6] If the man is on land, the block of wood will fall to the ground. If the man is in the International Space Station, it will float weightlessly. If the man is under water, it will float up to the surface. Assume nothing!

[7] The dead bodies are fish. They were swimming in an aquarium when the cat knocked the tank onto the floor when he tried to get at the fish and eat them. The tank crashed onto the floor. The cat got scared and ran away.

[8] Night watchmen have no business dreaming at night. They're supposed to keep awake while on duty.

[9] The proposed identity test was a simple blood test. The magistrate knew that the true heir would never have agreed to such a test, because the family in question was well known to carry a strain of hemophilia and for a hemophiliac (or bleeder) even a small scratch is a terrifying, and potentially fatal, prospect.

[10] He juggled the cantaloupes.

[11] The German owns the fish, and the following details the full answer:

Nationality: Norwegian, Dane, Brit, German, Swede

Color: yellow, blue, red, green, white

Beverage: water, tea, milk, coffee, beer

Smokes: Dunhill, Blend, Pall Mall, Prince, Blue Master

Pet: cats, horses, birds, fish, dogs

I once worked with two creative people, both of whom I admired and respected enormously. I'll call them Jack and Jill. Both were brilliant. Both could generate a hundred different ideas in the blink of an eye. Some of which were brilliant. Most of which were wonderful. Few of which were pedestrian in any way, shape, or form.

Jack and Jill were so much alike.

And yet they were so different.

Jack was the consummate outside-the-box thinker. Nobody I had ever met had his ability to reach into odd places and pull out strange and wonderful and mind-poppingly ingenious ideas.

But the moment that Jack met with resistance, the second that he ran up against the slightest constraint, he would go completely and totally ballistic. He would argue over the smallest of things. Dumb things. Things that just didn't matter. If someone had a reason why he couldn't say something, Jack would fight to the death to say it anyway. Jack refused to accept anything that impeded his thinking. One day, in a presentation to a client, he finally lost it when he picked up his half-empty cup of coffee and threw it across the conference room table at the client. Jack was never seen or heard from again.

And then there was Jill.

Like Jack, Jill was a creative genius, and she had the awards to prove it. Throughout the advertising business, her talents were the stuff of legend. There wasn't an agency in the country that wouldn't have hired her if they could.

But unlike Jack, Jill was undeterred by constraints. She didn't like them necessarily. No one does. But she accepted them as a reality. And because she did, Jill was very good at thinking inside the box, the very place where Jack had eventually met his professional doom.

Jill would take her ideas to the client. Sometimes the client would love what Jill had done. But at other times the client would say things like, "It feels too edgy" or "I don't like funny radio commercials" or "Does it really have to be shot in Patagonia?"

Like a boxer, Jill could take a punch. Jill could take a *lot* of punches. And yet no matter what happened, Jill would listen, she would go back to her office, and she would reshape and rejigger, retool and reinvent, all the while refusing to return to the client with something less than wonderful.

It might have taken her ten tries. It might have taken her a hundred. It didn't matter. Jill just accepted the ebbs and flows of the process, threaded the conceptual needle, and eventually ended up with work that everyone agreed was a winner.

Jack was creative.

Jill was creative.

But Jack was delusional. He refused to accept that advertising, like everything else in life, is a box. Jill, on the other hand, looked at the creative process and saw a river strewn with boulders and downed trees and yet navigable. Jack didn't. Brilliant as he was, he balked at limitations. The very thought of not only accepting constraints but embracing them was utterly repugnant to him. He insisted on thinking in a vacuum, and it didn't work.

Limitations are a good thing. They give us direction. They point us toward something instead of toward nothing. They channel our creative energy and give it meaning. And if we can only learn to use them to our advantage, we are all capable of immense imagination.

Jill learned this.

I hope you will, too.

Adforum.com, 91–92

Advanced Media Products, 151–52

Amabile, T. M., 69

American Institute of Certified Public Accountants (AICPA), 35–36

Ammirati & Puris, 70–72

Angel's advocates, 170–71

Antonym lens, 167–68

Apollo 13 flight, as example of Houdini Solution, 9–10

Apple Computer
innovation and, 30
"1984" commercial, 85–86

Asking "why," 188–89

Association
free, 179
restricting free, 179–80

Assumption blindness, 187–88

Bagnall, Jim, 114

Bang & Olufsen, 14–15

Barriers. *See also* Limits to creativity
"all I know is, it worked before" myth, 43–45
"bigger the budget, bigger the idea" myth, 49–50
"creativity is for creative people" myth, 34–36
"devil's advocate or idea assassin" myth, 40–41
"grapes can die on the vine; so can a great idea" myth, 38–40
"if it walks like a duck" myth, 50–51
"in life, and in business, no one can hear you scream" myth, 48–49

"only good idea is a big idea" myth, 41–43

"so little time, so few ideas" myth, 49

"that's why they call it work" myth, 36–38

"there's no such thing as an original idea" myth, 51–52

"we don't need no stinking questions" myth, 46–47

"we have our way of doing things" myth, 51

"you can't rock the world if you don't rock the boat" myth, 45–46

creativity and, 217

fear of, 28–31

Batman, 39

Bay, Michael, 55

BBDO, 196–97

Behavioral profiling, 109–11

Bélec, Anne E., 18

Bernoulli, Daniel, 158–59

Bey, Rahman, 26–27

Biases, overcoming ingrained, exercise for, 206–7

Big ideas. *See also* Ideas; Small ideas

competition and, 158

creativity and, 148

expectations and, 156–57

money and, 103–7

vs. small ideas, 41–43

time and, 207–8

Blair Witch Project, The, 12–14

Blinders, for limiting distractions, 79–81

Boardroom Inc., 42–43

Boldyrev, Dmitry, 151–52

"Bottles and knives" puzzle, 192

Bowie, David, 22

Box, life as a, 3–6

Boxes. *See also* Limits

boxes inside, 174–75

bringing in fresh eyes for looking inside, 173–74

rolling walls of, 172–73

thinking inside, 53–54

Bradbury, Ray, 20, 177

Brainstorming, 196–97

Brandenburg, Karl-Heinz, 151

BRC Imagination Arts, 145

Breakthrough ideas, 153–55. *See also* Ideas

"Bridge Too Far" puzzle, 211

Brighthouse, 173

Brown, Rita Mae, 69

Brutethink, 180–81

Budgets. *See also* Money

creativity and, 87–92

ideas and, 98–99

Bulletproofing ideas, 170–71

Busch, Kyle, 81–82

Butler Shine & Stern, 155–56

Cannes International Advertising Festival, 91

Carrington, Hereward, 25–26

Carroll, Lewis, 184–85

Catalyst Ranch, 144–45

Chain Reaction Machine Challenge, 135–37

Change
creativity and, 58–59
fear of, 65–66

Chapman, Colin, 158–59

Chatterbox part, of human psyche, 56–57

Chess, thinking-inside-the-box creativity and, 204–5

Chevys restaurants, 11–12

Chiat/Day, 85–86

Children, creativity and, 127–31

Cinemasports, 73–74

"Circling the Story" game, for creative ideas, 181–82

Coca-Cola, 31–33, 40

"Coldest Day" exercise, 208

Collaboration, 153–55

Comfort zones, creativity and, 59

Connections, being forced to make, 113–15

Connors, Jack, 36–37

Converse Gallery, 155–56

Cosmopulos, Stavros, 78–79

Crandon, Margery, 25–26

Creative briefs, 78, 171

Creative people, resiliency and, 205–6

Creative restraints, power of, 21–23

Creative visual thinking, exercise for, 196

Creativity, 87–92. *See also* Innovation
barriers to, 217
"all I know is, it worked before" myth, 43–45
"bigger the budget, bigger the idea" myth, 49–50
"creativity is for creative people" myth, 34–36
"devil's advocate or idea assassin" myth, 40–41
"grapes can die on the vine; so can a great idea" myth, 38–40
"if it walks like a duck" myth, 50–51
"in life, and in business, no one can hear you scream" myth, 48–49
"only good idea is a big idea" myth, 41–43
"so little time, so few ideas" myth, 49
"that's why they call it work" myth, 36–38
"there's no such thing as an original idea" myth, 51–52
"we don't need no stinking questions" myth, 46–47

"we have our way of doing things" myth, 51

"you can't rock the world if you don't rock the boat" myth, 45–46

big ideas and, 148

budgets and, 87–92

change and, 58–59

children and, 127–31

deadlines and, 69–77

as destructive act, 31–34, 58–59

fear and. *See* Fears

going beyond preconceptions and, 118–23

guarantees and, 31–33

learning, 166–67

limits and, 6–8

money and, 87–92, 95–98

as nuclear reactor, 15–19, 47

play and, 132–35

stagnation and, 33

steps for, 104–7

steps to take to encourage, with deadlines, 77–86

ensuring ideas work right out of the box, 85–86

limiting distractions, 79–81

limiting number of people involved in projects, 82–85

setting single objectives, 77–79

using experienced people, 81–82

Creativity sanctuaries, 145

Da Vinci, Leonardo, 212–15

Darwin's Theory of Innovation, 112–15

de Bono, Edward, 188, 191

Deadlines

creativity and, 69–77

steps to take to encourage creativity with, 77–86

ensuring ideas work right out of the box, 85–86

limiting distractions, 79–81

limiting number of people involved in projects, 82–85

setting single objectives, 77–79

using experienced people, 81–82

Devil's advocates, 40–41, 170–71

Dietzgen, 112–13

Disney, Walt, 93–95, 103

Distractions, limiting, 79–81

Dogme Manifesto, 100–103

Dominoes, Kipling's, 211–12

"Dream Sequence" puzzle, 209–10

Dundon, Elaine, 46

Eiger Labs, 152

Einstein, Five Houses of, 216–17

Eliot, T. S., 25
Emotional Quotient, choosing
    people with high, 106–7
Eno, Brian, 22
Enstein, Albert, 216
Entebbe raid, 77–78
Experience, for deadlines and
    creativity, 81–82

Fact Matrix, 200–202
Failing, fear of, 64–65
Fallon, Pat, 84
Fallon McElligott Rice, 84,
    96–97, 103
Fears
    of barriers, 28–31
    creativity and, 29–30, 61–64
    rational vs. irrational, 48–49
    that keep one from being
        creative
        fear of change, 65–66
        fear of failing, 64–65
        fear of going broke, 66–67
        fear of succeeding, 65
        fear of time, 67–68
FedEx, 71, 188
Ferentz, Tom, 88
Fincher, David, 55
"Finding the gold" exercise,
    192–93
Firefox, 155
Fischli, Peter, 149–50
Five Houses of Einstein, 216–17
Flexibility, 19–21

Frankel, Justin, 151–52
Fraunhofer Institut Integrierte
    Schaltungen, 151
Free association, 179
    restricting, 179–80
"Fugitive, The" puzzle, 192

Gehry, Frank, 38
Gerhard, Susan, 102
Gibson, William, 39
Gladwell, Malcolm, 106
Going broke, fear of, 66–67
Going into other peoples' minds,
    exercise for, 190–91
Goodby Berlin Silverstein, 11–12
Gordon, Jeff, 81–82
Grant, Charles L., 81
Gregory, Kathryn, 137–38
Grisham, John, 67–68
Groundbreaking ideas, being
    ready for, 162–64. *See also*
    Ideas
Groups, problem solving and,
    153–55

Hadley, C. N., 69
Hakuta, Ken, 87
Hatch Awards, 57
"Heir apparent" puzzle, 210–11
Higher Self part, of human psy-
    che, 67–68
Hoberman, J., 102–3
Hollywood, thinking in the box
    and, 5

Holmes, Oliver Wendell, 147
Houdini, Harry, 1–2, 25–28
Houdini Solution, 8
   Apollo 13 flight as example of,
      9–10
   barriers and, 145
   as creative judo, 11–12
   defined, 2
   flexibility and, 19–21
   New Zealand as example of,
      4–5
Houdini thinkers, 19–21
Hubbard, Gardiner Greene, 113
Human psyche, parts of, 56–57

Ideas, 163–64. *See also* Big ideas;
   Small ideas
   being ready for groundbreak-
      ing, 162–64
   big vs. small, 41–43
   breakthrough, 153–55
   budgets and, 98–99
   bulletproofing, 170–71
   "Circling the Story" game, for
      creating, 181–82
   dealing with unworkable,
      175–76
   groundbreaking, 162–64
   money and, 103–7
   profiling, 50–51
   transplanting, 148–53
IDEO, 131–34, 143
Illustrated Man, The (Bradbury),
   20–21

Imagination, childhood and,
   127–31
Innovation. *See also* Creativity
   Apple Computer
      and, 30
   Darwin's Theory of,
      112–15
Inspiration, finding, technique
   for, 215–16
Intelligence, emotional vs.
   intellectual, 106–7
iPod, 152, 159–60
Irrational fear, 48–49

Jeffers, Susan, 56
Jobs, Steve, 30, 152
Johnson, Kelly, 83

Kamen, Dean, 157
Kamler, Kenneth, 57–58
Katell, Dave, 189
Kaye, Tony, 55
Keller, Helen, 64
Kelley, Tom, 132
Kim, W. Chan, 158
King, Stephen, 81
Kipling's Dominoes, 211–12
Koberg, Don, 114
Krakauer, Jon, 57
Kramer, S. J., 69

Left-brain thinkers, 85–86
Leibowitz, Annie, 89
Leonard, Joshua, 14

Leonard Monahan Saabye, 56, 142–43
Life, as a box, 3–6
Limits. *See also* Barriers
  creativity and, 6–8
  inventing, 21–22
  as liberators, 12–15
  test for, 185–86
Lin, Maya, 122
Linde, Andrei, 73
Linux, 154–55
Lockheed Martin, 82–83
Lollicata, Russell, 63
Luminaries, 173

Madison Avenue, thinking in the box and, 5
Magnetism, creative, 189–90
Martin Agency, 90
MasterCard's "Priceless" campaign, exercise for, 193–95
Mauborgne, Renée, 158
May, Rollo, 6
McCurry, Steve, 89
McElligott, Tom, 84
McKee, Robert, 5
Meetings, creativity and, 80–81
Member, Maxwell, 53
Metaphors, finding, 177–79
Michalko, Michael, 180–81
Michelangelo, 1
Moffett, Mark, 71
Monahan, Tom, 75, 76

Money. *See also* Budgets
  Walt Disney and, 93–95
  big ideas and, 103–7
  creativity and, 87–92, 95–98
Morphological forced connections, 114–15
Mountain bikes, 156–57
Movie industry, 99–100
MP3 player, 151–52
Murder mystery exercise, 209
Myrick, Daniel, 12–13
Myths, about creativity
  "all I know is, it worked before," 43–45
  "bigger the budget, bigger the idea," 49–50
  "creativity is for creative people," 34–36
  "devil's advocate or idea assassin," 40–41
  "grapes can die on the vine; so can a great idea," 38–40
  "if it walks like a duck," 50–51
  "in life, and in business, no one can hear you scream," 48–49
  "only good idea is big idea," 41–43
  "so little time, so few ideas," 49
  "that's why they call it work," 36–38
  "there's no such thing as an original idea," 51–52

"we don't need no sticking
    questions," 46–47
"we have our way of doing
    things," 51
"you can't rock the world if
    you don't rock the boat,"
    45–46

Narcissists, 106
Nash, John, 73
Neuromancer (Gibson), 39
New Zealand, 4–5
Newton, Sir Isaac, 130–31
Nike, 38

Objectives, single, 77–79
Oblique Strategies, 22
Obstacles. *See* Limits
Oklahoma City National
    Memorial, 123
One-trick ponies, 43–45
Onion, peeling the, 104–5
Opportunities, Houdini compa-
    nies and, 19–21
Orton, William, 113, 116
Osborne, Fred, 196–97
Osman, Dan, 63

Palo Alto Research Center
    (PARC), 30
Peeling the onion, 104–5
Pepsi, 31–32
Picasso, Pablo, 127
Pilkington, Alastair, 115–16

Play. *See also* Work
    creating off-site workplaces
        for, 143–46
    creativity and, 132–41
    starting companies and,
        141–43
Play (corporation), 132–33, 143
Poetry jams, 208–9
Polaroid, 30–31
Ponies, one-trick, 43–45
Preconceptions, 109–11, 117–18
    going beyond, 118–23
"Priceless" campaign,
        MasterCard's, exercise for,
        193–95
Problem solving
    groups and, 153–55
    through back door, 183
Problems, shrinking, 171–72
Profiling ideas, 50–51
Psyche, human, parts of, 56–57

Questions
    asking the right, 15–16
    creative thinkers and, 46–47
    myth about, 46–47

Rational fear, 48–49
Reiman, Joey, 173
Remembrance technique, 202–3
Resiliency, creative people and,
        205–6
Restraints, power of creative,
        21–23. *See also* Limits

Rice, Anne, 39
Rice, Nancy, 84
Ripomatic, 183–84
Risk, 45–46
Robinson, Alan G., 42
Roosevelt, Franklin D., 61
Rudd, Tony, 158–59
Rutan, Burt, 124–25

Sànchez, Eduardo, 12–13
Sanctuaries, creativity, 145
Sand box puzzle, 185
Santa Cruz Film Festival, 73–74
SCAMPER technique, 197–200
Scherfig, Lone, 102
Schroeder, Dean M., 42
Segway HT, 157–58
Seitzer, Dieter, 151
Sidewinder missiles, 216
Silveira, Mark, 71, 72, 76
Simon, Paul, 43
Simpson, Steve, 11–12, 19
Single objectives, 77–79
Single-minded points, 77–79
Sixth Street Photography
    Workshop (SSPW), 88–89,
    104
Skunk Works, 82–83
Sloan, Paul, 188
Small ideas. See also Big ideas;
    Ideas
    advantages of, 159–61, 163–64
    vs. big ideas, 41–43
Smith, Fred, 188

Smith, Patrick, 150
Smylie, Ed, 9–10
Snowballing, 169
SolutionPeople, 144
Sorkin, Aaron, 191
Space, defining one's, 104
Stagnation, creativity and, 33
Storyboarding, 183–84
Strategies, Oblique, 22
Succeeding, fear of, 65
Sullivan, Luke, 90
Surowiecki, James, 153–54
Swigert, Jack, 9

Tarsem, 55
Thinking
    exercise for creative visual, 196
    fast, 105–6
    inside the box, 5, 53–54
    wide-angle, 176–77
Thinkubator, 144–45
Time
    big ideas and, 207–8
    fear of, 67–68

United Parcel Service (UPS),
    70–72
Unworkable ideas, dealing with,
    175–76
Uzelac, Tomislav, 151

Vick, Ed, 72
Vietnam Veterans Memorial,
    Washington, DC, 121–23

Vinterberg, Thomas, 99–103
Visual thinking, exercise for creative, 196
Volvo, 16–18
von Trier, Lars, 99–103

"Walking the line" exercises, 195
Walls. *See also* Limits
    rolling, 172–73
    understanding, 33–34
Weiss, David, 149–50
Wells, H. G., 43
Welsh, Jack, 75
Western Union, 112–13

"What Is It?" puzzle, 191
White, Jack, 21–23
"Why," asking, 188–89
Wide-angle thinking, 176–77
Wieden+Kennedy, 38, 149–50
Williamson, Marianne, 65
Wong, Tracy, 11–12, 19
Word racing, 186–87
Work, 138–39. *See also* Play
Wright, Peter, 158–59

Xerox, 30

Zyman, Sergio, 32